One Woman's Love Affair with the Magic, Music and Men of Cuba

The Breath of Cuba: Part 2

Passion Play

Cheri Shanti

The Breath of Cuba Part II: Passion Play
Copyright © 2020 Cheri Shanti

ISBN #: 978-0-9995275-2-8
Kindle EBook ISBN: 978-0-9995275-3-5

Table of Contents

To The Dance

There is nothing else
but this bliss
Everything in between is waiting
for you to return

I am nothing without you
You are my everything
My heart
My soul
My reason to be

You are my passion, my purpose
My life, my death
My remembrance of who I am
My place to forget the illusions

Before you and after you
I am dead

In your embrace
I come alive
Singing incantations of desire
Prophesying the truths of truths
I am
Always effortlessly in motion

Beyond time
I am yours
Beyond form
I am yours

I can never forsake you
No man can hold me
Until he has found me here
With your arms around me
Embraced together
In the rhythms of all time
Lost forever in the magic
That finds souls merging
in this love

You are my desire
My call, my response
And in you
I am free
Forever more

Author's Foreword: An Introduction to Part 2

The Breath of Cuba: Part II, is a continuation of a love affair with Cuba that began for me many years ago. If you have come across this book, and you have not read Part I, I encourage you to read it. Part I tells my story of the first time I went to Cuba to study the music of the religion of Santería and its rhythms. Through the journey, I gained a new appreciation for my story. I was able to see how sharing my story impacted others, both in Cuba and in my own country. I discovered my own humanity, in all its glory and nasty grit, in profound and humbling ways. I went to study the drum, and found myself falling deeply in love with the culture, the people, and the lifestyle. I discovered a way of life that was foreign to me, but that strangely resonated with a part of my soul that was unfed in my own culture.

My life has not been the same since. Cuba healed something in me that I did not even know needed healing. Its magic continues to work in my life every day.

I have deliberated for some time about publishing this second part of my story. Naturally, many of my perspectives shifted between Parts I and II, and even more of them have shifted since this story was originally documented as my personal memoirs in 2012.

In 2017, I sold everything I owned, left the USA, and committed to spending as much time as I possibly could in Cuba. I ended up being there for the better part of three years with only short visits to the USA, primarily for visa renewals. I lived mostly in Trinidad, Cuba. After living inside of the culture in this way, naturally, my understanding is much more vast than it was in the early years of my journeys in Cuba in which Parts I and II took place.

The Breath of Cuba story comes from my memoirs, and as such, it is quite intimate. My intention is to give you glimpses into a culture that is often as mysterious to the Cubans themselves as it is to outsiders who may be trying to understand its complexity.

Part II: Passion Play will take you deeper into Cuba, primarily through the lens of relationships. Cuban relationships are complex, mysterious and often marked with intense drama. Cubans love deeply, and passionately. The machismo of the Latin culture can create challenging dynamics in cross cultural relationships, such as those I entered into as an American woman. In spite of drama and appearances, Cubans have a very straightforward, down-to-earth understanding of humanity. This allows them the ability to maintain and evolve relationships throughout the different cycles of life and demonstrates an unconditional love that lies at the heart of their culture.

As I prefaced in Part I, it is important that I speak to the fact that I do not in any way address politics or the social structures that are in place in Cuba. This is a personal story, and not tied to any kind of political inclination whatsoever. My opinions and perspectives are just that, my opinions and perspectives. Clearly, I can never even begin to understand what it is like to be a Cuban living in Cuba having gone through what many Cuban people have endured to survive. As a white woman from the USA, I am also well aware that I am granted certain privileges, as well as restrictions while in Cuba. I am also aware that, while I can do my best to understand and translate, sometimes what I share may not always be perfectly accurate interpretations.

Cuban life, for the average Cuban, is incredibly challenging on many levels. There are issues there that even many Cubans themselves will tell you they do not understand, especially in regard to politics and economics. I do not subscribe to any certain ideology or political viewpoint. I am not in any way here to say what is right or wrong.

Cuba is Cuba. For any visitor to go there and expect it to function the same as other places is like biting into an apple and expecting it to taste like a banana. Certainly, there is much to be learned from the way the people have adapted to challenging situations with their humanity so intact. My love affair with Cuba has nothing to do with politics or economics; yet I realize that everything Cuban is a result of the unique impacts that politics and economics have had. I am in love with the island, its people, its music, and culture. I am not blind to its struggles, nor to the issues of human rights, nor am I ignorant to the impacts that the political system has had on the people. I simply chose not to write about it, because not only is it highly controversial, it is also a complicated and multifaceted conversation that even most Cubans are not able to fully comprehend. I do not feel anywhere near competent enough to write about these complex issues.

Part II starts at the beginning of my second trip to Cuba. I went through what I can only liken to a type of withdrawal symptom after leaving Cuba the first time. I drifted in and out of depression. I found myself missing something that I had discovered in Cuba that I couldn't seem to find in my life in the USA. When I got the opportunity to return, and with a Cuban by my side, I jumped at it!

Many people experience culture shock when leaving their own culture. I have always experienced more of a reverse culture shock upon *returning to my own culture.* In the time between my first and second trip, I deeply missed the simplicity of integrated village life. I found I longed for the time away from technology that Cuba offered me.

I am old enough to recall a time before cell phones and personal laptops. I remember the mystery of life before constant contact, instant messaging and facetime. I remember the feeling of having total freedom from anyone being able to reach me. I remember the sense of adventure it brought to my life. I much prefer the magic and mystery of natural living, to the overstimulated, constant beeping, buzzing and neurosis that technology seems to breed. Cuba gave me an opportunity to remember the spontaneous magic of life. Being away from it, my soul simply craved more of it.

There seems to now be an unspoken, but clearly understood, expectation that we should always be available, always respond immediately, and always be within an arm's reach of our mobile devices. Personal space and privacy can be interrupted at any time by the beeping or vibration of these devices. The sense of obligation to play the game is, in reality, much more than just a sense of obligation. It is becoming increasingly difficult to survive in the modern world without a mobile device and an almost constant internet connection. Banking, business, shopping, and almost all communications now are dependent on how connected you are.

The direction of more, faster, better, for me, has only served to make me feel more stressed, faster to feel unwell, and better off as far away from it all as I can manage to stay. Finding a world that, in 2012, still had not yet become fully connected, allowed me to revisit the mystery life can offer. I was able to remember that synchronicities and magic are constantly available in the world away from cyberspace. It had a huge impact on my heart, mind and humanity. I wanted more.

During the time between Parts I and II, while in the USA, I did everything I could to bring a little of Cuba into my life in order to cope. I kept the promise I made to myself to learn to dance salsa. What I learned of family and community in Cuba, I sought to bring into my daily life, from house parties, to randomly stopping by to see friends, and prioritizing my family more. In short, I was constantly trying to get back to something that I had tasted in Cuba.

In spite of all my attempts to sink back into my life in the USA, the dream of Cuba lived on. I continued to have visions of myself there. I would often see myself sitting on the rock in Cojimar that I often frequented by the sea to meditate. The dream of returning, and of finding some way to stay longer, never left me. Clearly there was something more for me there. I knew that I would find a way to get back again, when the time was right.

I was sure that a second trip would break the spell. A second trip would allow me to finally get back to being happy with the life that I had been creating for so many years in my own country.

During this time, I had very little interest in men or dating. Something in me had closed down completely from all the trauma I had experienced from my previous partner. More and more so, I was quite content alone. In fact, I began to fully enjoy being single. I gave up on trying to fix me, and just let myself be me. I had cried all I could cry, and processed all I could process. It had become time to allow time to do its work. I used it as an opportunity to explore new ways of sharing through community and dancing that did not require such a heavy emotional investment.

The world of salsa dancing became my medicine, my therapy and my social life. It also became my playground for new paradigms in relationships. Like drumming, salsa dancing became a personal sanctuary from the mundane. It was my own very intimate rhythm church. I discovered that on the dance floor, I had full permission to express my sensuality safely, without any expectation of sex or the disappointment of failed relationships. I could touch the divinity within and around me in the dance. I discovered a new form of intimacy in the arms of countless men swirling me on the dance floor into my bliss. It was powerfully alluring and addictive. I fell in love with this world: a world where a man and a woman can move passionately and sensually together, in a rhythmic embrace, then walk away smiling, with no harm done, no words exchanged, and moments of supreme pleasure shared.

It wasn't long after I started to learn to dance that I found myself out five or six nights a week, feeding my new addiction with endless hours on the dance floor. I was committed that when I did return to Cuba, I would never again have to feel like the two-left-footed dork that I had felt like when I was there before. I wanted to go back with a level of mastery that only comes from hours of practice. My drumming began to be less and less a part of my life, as the dance took me over. It quickly became my most passionate and joyous expression.

In the dance, I felt like I could be celebrated as my most sensual, playful and creative self. It was less cerebral and more feminine than drumming. It forced me to surrender in order to be led. I learned to love that I did not always have to be in control. If I was going to become a really good dancer, I had to completely let go of being in control. I had to trust my partner. After just going through a break up that destroyed my trust in men completely, I found that the dance began to slowly restore my ability to trust. It was through the dance that my heart began to soften, slowly and quietly. Through the dance, I found a new community of friends, many of whom were Latino, which I found comforting with my broken cultural identity crisis of being a white American woman who has always felt totally out of place in her own culture.

Some months after I had started dancing more seriously, I went to see a live salsa band. Late in the night, a black man, dressed in pure white from head to toe crossed my field of vision. For the first time in almost three years, I felt a stirring within me. I was captivated by him and powerfully attracted. Everything about him intrigued me: the stark contrast of the whites he wore against his dark skin. The way he walked with a swagger that bordered on a limp. The pure animalistic sensuality that poured through him. The way he danced with a casual mastery that I had never seen before: it all captivated me. I knew nothing about him. All I knew was that I wanted to become a good enough dancer to be able to meet him on the dance floor with confidence.

It was a few months later at another event in a neighboring city that I saw him again, and a few months after that that he finally asked me to dance. I was nervous to accept his hand, afraid my two left feet would return and that I would become a fumbling mess of apologies for being clumsy or off time. It was quite the opposite. I felt secure, lifted, cherished and held. The chemistry between us was undeniable, and almost overwhelming. His dancing was a new world for me. He was simultaneously soft and strong. I felt masterfully guided and supported, but he was never pushy, flashy or overdone. He had a relaxed mastery that I did not experience in most of the dancers I had come to know. I could feel that he had been dancing his entire life.

At the end of the dance, he said, "Wow, you dance very well." I soon discovered that he was Cuban, and he soon discovered my love affair with his country. Over the course of the following months, he and I developed a friendship that turned into a steamy love affair, with Cuba right in the middle of it all.

One night sitting on my porch overlooking the lake, he invited me to go to Cuba with him. I, of course, said yes. This is where Part II begins.

Love never points a finger to say what is right or wrong. Love accepts and seeks to understand, and ultimately, love is about the unfolding of the heart. Cuba has played a huge role in unfolding mine, and in teaching me about my own humanity, about relationships, and mostly about the power of unconditional love. It is this experience of love that I long to share with you.

I hope you enjoy the story. I love hearing from my readers, please feel free to contact me through the website at www.thebreathofcuba.com.

All names in Part II have been changed to protect the privacy of my friends and beloved in this story.

The Return

The tires of the plane hit the ground, and the plane erupts into a joyous yip. Already the expressive spirit of this island is singing through me. We have arrived in Cuba. I feel a delicious sense of coming home. It feels warm and welcoming, and just slightly tinged with the surreal quality of mystery and the unknown. When I left Cuba a few years ago, I had no doubt that I would someday return. The feeling of walking into a dream, is powerful as the plane rolls towards the airport filled with happy chattering Cubans.

My Cuban lover sits next to me. He touches my hand lightly and smiles. I want to devour him right now in gratitude for inviting me to meet his family and have a more intimate gateway to the culture. His work has had him traveling for the past few weeks, and this is the first time we've seen each other for some time. I am excited for the moment when I can pull him close to me to incite his incantations of primal passion in his homeland.

The airport looks bleak and uninviting, almost intimidating. There is a soft haze spreading across the tarmac. I know that beyond that stagnant illusion lies a world of magic, music and men awaiting me, and for that I am excited. There is so much that has changed within me since the last time I came to this island. I smile inwardly reflecting on the growth that has come in two years of being single.

My lover's strong black hand grasps my thigh with ardor as I lay my head back against the seat. His passion burns right into me through his hands. My body softens and tingles in anticipation for his lips on my skin. Carlos is my first Cuban lover. I am quite sure that he will not be my last. Closing my eyes briefly, I reflect on the movie of memories in my mind of my last trip to this rhythmical rock. I was so shut down to men, intimacy or any kind of romantic connection when I was in Cuba last time. Yet, I remember the sensations that were roused here all too well. The intoxicating passion and desire that the men stirred in me just passing them on the streets as they looked through me. The heat their eyes could well up from inside of me, despite my walls and defenses.

I am most definitely a very different woman now than I was then. I find myself excited by new possibilities and new ways I will get to experience Cuba because of the work I've been doing on my heart, body and mind. In the past two years, I have shed layer after layer of my conditioning, fears, insecurities and social pretenses. I have uncovered the essence of the wild woman within me as much as the wise one. It has been a journey of ripping away the soul-suffocating stories that my culture taught me of how a woman should behave to be respectable, proper and socially accepted. I have found peace with my emotional self as well as my rational logical self. I have delved deep into the sensual stirrings of my femininity and granted them full permission to find enjoyment in men, whom I once would have been afraid to consider, because of the social and cultural stigmas I once learned. I stomped out the prude in me, and claimed my sensuality and sexuality as a natural part of my being. I faced the untamed, wild, warrior woman within me with eyes wide open, peering steadfast into the darkness. I learned to love the pleasure and wisdom that she can invite.

I found that at forty years old, there was an insatiable sexual hunger burning in me that I had never felt. I found pleasure in the lip licking lust that it birthed in me. I grew to understand the younger man's fascination with the mature woman, and vice versa. I found myself exploring the nights alone, contemplating the deeper worlds of my own inner sexuality in quiet observation of the thoughts and impulses that were flowing through me. I learned that my feline intuitive wisdom as a woman also blesses me with clear discernment on which men to steer clear of, and which ones are safe.

In learning to dance salsa and how to be led by a male partner, I discovered that dancing empowered me to enjoy intimacy without sexuality. I discovered that I had been hiding certain parts of myself out of a fear of the power of that feline intuition and desire. I consciously kicked all my old conditioning of what it meant to be a woman to the curb and set myself free. My inhibitions and stories about what was "ok" for me as a woman were crushed by the overpowering need to be real with what I was feeling, and to find the truth of myself on all levels. I let myself feel, react, respond and be authentic in my expressions in every way. I stopped caring about what anyone else would think, and let myself follow my desires. In short, I began having more fun than ever before.

The result is that I have found infinite grace pouring through me in every moment that is mine to claim. I jumped into full acceptance of being and loving myself exactly as I am with no holds barred. I stood naked with myself and hurled a stone of intent at the mirrors of my mind's conditioning. I let all the illusions shatter, standing fearlessly in the unveiling of both the wild and the wise within me, as the shards fell to the ground in a cacophony of simultaneous destruction and creation.

Most importantly perhaps, I committed that I would never again lose myself in the arms and illusions of a man's love. I decided that being single offered me tremendous freedom and opportunity. It allows me to create my life on my own terms, and to live my dreams fully. I committed that I would not compromise what I want in a relationship just to be with someone, no matter how wonderful it appeared to be at the onset. I came to terms with the reality that I was dangerously attracted to bad boys with bulging biceps and rock hard bodies, but that didn't mean I had to put myself in the line of danger to appreciate what they could offer me on or off of the dance floor. I learned to be fully alive and to be empowered by owning my desire for sensual, soul-merging sex. I discovered that there is actually something incredibly liberating about two adults with no drama, no stories, and no emotional baggage giving themselves fully to each other for shared healing and fun.

I have faced loneliness, depression and my own deep fears of unworthiness, and accepted that they are companions I will walk this life with forever. I befriended them as my allies to deeper understandings. I no longer fear them or run from them. As Ram Dass once said of his neurosis, "I invite them in for tea." In short, I got real with myself and found that I can love and accept all of myself. I redefined for myself what it meant to be a liberated, empowered woman at middle age. I found that I could feel sexier, more alive and happier the more I accepted myself without judgment. I found peace in accepting my imperfections and humanity on all levels.

I am brought back to the moment as soft, full lips brush my ear. I feel my lover's hot breath whispering to me. Before I even hear the words, my body stirs in response to the warmth of his breath.

"Baby, te quiero, no puedo esperar para ti." His tongue lightly tickles my ear and I want only him. I say nothing and simply smile. "Vamos," he says and we are in motion, grabbing bags and filing off the plane.

He slaps my ass lightly on the way out of the plane. I feel a pleasant jolt of desire stir within me. I am smiling in joyous delight as we walk onto the tarmac and Cuba's hot, steamy, pungent air greets my senses.

The Breath of Cuba stirs in me again.

La Familia

A few hours later, I find myself in a taxi heading to Carlos's sister's home for dinner. I am following my lover's lead and grateful to not be left alone quite yet. I know that I am safe and that the most important part of this journey is trusting and being open to the journey as it unfolds.

I do my best to try to remember how and when to roll my r's and how to understand Cuban Spanish at warp speed. Stark imagery greets my eyes. I love the nostalgia of the old cars, the horse-drawn carts, and the weathered faces of the Cuban cowboys with fat cigars hanging from their parched lips. I even love the stench that lingers like a heavy pudding in the air. It is a smell I have come to know as distinctly Cuban.

When we arrive at the house, Carlos's family members all greet me with hugs and kisses and welcome me in as part of the family. This familial warmth that was so naturally extended to me, even as a total stranger, is at the heart of Cuba's allure for me. The house is a two story concrete structure with peeling paint and metal-barred windows. It is typical of those found in the barrios of Havana, away from the historic center. The whole family lives there together. Carlos's sister, her husband, and their kids live upstairs and grandma has the downstairs house.

His grandmother sits on the front porch smiling for no apparent reason. An unlit, unlabeled, flaking cigar hangs softly from her wrinkly, toothless mouth. She sits perched up in a wheelchair in an aged white garment that shamelessly reveals her saggy breasts. Her eyes light up with joy when we step onto the porch. She reaches out to us to embrace us, and welcome us to her home. I feel like I am being greeted by someone who loves me with all her heart and has not seen me in years as the tears roll down her face when we embrace. I hug her and look deep into her dark watery eyes. I find myself in love with this woman instantly.

Upstairs, a feast has been prepared. Fresh sliced tomatoes and onion, a big bowl of rice, plates of chicken, fish, and bread are shared with enthusiastic conversations and lots of laughter. Within a few hours, inhibitions are fully dissolved as rum is passed freely, and the music is turned on. Instinctively my body moves to the rhythm. Carlos immediately takes my hand to show off my salsa skills to his family. They watch us move skillfully in the tiny living room with appreciative remarks and comments of disbelief that this white woman, who barely speaks Spanish, can actually dance.

When I was in Cuba the first time, I could not dance salsa. Not even a little bit. I was a dorky white woman who could not surrender to my partner's guidance to save my life. I was a bumbling disaster as a salsa partner. Looking back, I can admit that I was an overly controlling American woman who did not know how to be led. I got flustered the moment a man drew me into his arms to dance. On this first night back on the island of Cuba, guided by Carlos, I am now whirling about with ease, grace and confidence. Now I can dance with almost any level of dancer, and feel totally relaxed and receptive. In the midst of the spins with Carlos, I am giving myself inner high fives. I feel a deep sense of accomplishment that I took on the challenge of learning to dance salsa before returning to Cuba.

Learning to dance has taught me something far more valuable than just the dance itself. I have learned more about the intrinsic beauty of the masculine and feminine (or lead and follow) than I could have ever imagined. In salsa, the lead (masculine) role is that of leadership and initiative. On the esoteric level, this role is that of providing soft strength and in the highest forms of dance, a true endearment of the feminine (or follow). The best lead dancers are the ones who make their partners feel sexy, safe, and respected, while also challenging the follow to be strong in their own expression. A good lead knows how to show off a woman's natural beauty and sensuality and support her to shine. The metaphor of the dance for healthy balanced relationships has never been missed on me. In fact, learning the dance has completely transformed my relationships with men, with myself and with life itself.

Through the dance, I have softened, strengthened, refined and found empowerment in the sensuality that I love to express as a woman. I have learned how to be receptive, how to trust a man's leadership, and how to not only surrender to it, but to thoroughly enjoy the experience. I have also found new reserves of empowerment dancing with men who are powerful. They challenge me to anchor myself in the music with strength and sometimes even ferocity.

Dancing is a language in and of itself, and in Cuba it is *not* reserved for romance in any way. It is a way of sharing humanity and life. Everyone dances with everyone. There are no boundaries around who you can and can not dance with. In the dance, all are received equally with total joy. Men dance with men, women with women. Parents with their children, aunts, uncles, grandparents with children, it does not matter. It is all an expression of shared humanity.

More family members come throughout the night. The living room is small, intimate and packed to capacity. Being a newcomer, I am passed from Carlos to his cousin, to his uncle, to his brother-in-law, then to the other uncle, on and on and back to Carlos eventually. The women sit and watch my feet, talking amongst themselves in lightning fast Spanish, all the while offering appreciative smiles and nods of acknowledgement. They occasionally get up and join the dancing too.

This is the Cuban way. Sharing music, rum, and dancing in living rooms with family and friends is an integral part of Cuban culture. I find myself once again feeling that sense of belonging and family here that I rarely have felt in my own family. I can not help but make the mental note that I have never shared a dance with anyone in my blood family. A wave of grief washes over me as the rum sinks in with this awareness.

This is something I will never have in my own culture or family. I can only borrow it here, and experience it in this way, with people who are not blood relatives, but somehow are family of the heart.

I go outside and sit with Carlos's grandma on the porch. Out of nowhere, like a river busting through a dam after a long rain, the tears come. My first night back on this rock and the gravity of what I have been missing hits me. Grandma just smiles through her cigar and nods her head. I know she is feeling me somehow in her age and wisdom. I feel safe and comforted crying in front of this woman I just met a few hours ago. The rum is working on me, but it is only working to bring out the truth of what is.

Carlos's younger cousin, Yankel, comes down and embraces me. It doesn't strike me as strange or uncomfortable in any way. He feels like a little brother to me now after all the dancing and laughter upstairs. I feel safe, seen, and like I am with family. My heart is open. I feel a little raw and exposed through my tears, and yet completely accepted in my vulnerability.

"Que paso amiga?" he says as he sits down next to me. I let my head fall into his shoulder and try to explain my heart in my pathetic Spanish. He is patient and helps me with every word to speak correctly. He reminds me, in word and in heart, that family is not just about blood. Family is what we share as humanity in connection and understanding. Family is what we share through our hearts.

Carlos comes down the stairs as I am drying my tears. I instantly sense his jealousy. It surprises me, but I ignore it.

"What are you doing? Are you OK?" he says to me. I wipe the tears from my face and laugh as his cousin releases me.

"Yeah, I am good. I am so happy to be here. I have missed your island too much," I say.

"Come back upstairs. Come on, come on, you need to dance more." He takes my hand and leads me back to the party and we dance again. He was right. I needed to dance more. It snapped me right out of my grief and back into bliss.

After several more shots of rum and hours of dancing, I am exhausted. Carlos finds me, and brings me into one of the bedrooms, "Do you want to sleep here tonight or go with me to Havana now? I am taking my uncle and cousin back now. We can find you a room if you want." I am exhausted, and quite aware that he is likely drunk by now. Getting in a car with him does not sound inviting at all.

"I am so tired. Honestly baby, I do not want to go to Havana right now. I would love to stay here, but I don't know if it is OK." Not only was I tired, I was drunk and it was late. The thought of driving into Havana at this hour, to try to find a room was not a comforting one in any way. I wanted to be here, with him, and his family. I wanted us to be here, in his home, together for this first night in his homeland.

"You can stay here, but you know if you stay here, I am going to come in and make love to you when I come home." He said it so matter of factly, with such conviction that I was both amused and aroused. I took his face in my hands and kissed his lips passionately.

"Please, be safe and hurry back then." I said laughing, and pushed him out the door with a slap on his perfect booty.

Havana

Havana is a proud beautiful city even if it is in decay.
It breathes of an incredibly rich history filled with gambling, mobsters,
whores and em-passioned dreams that have been left to rot in the
shadows of Castro's reign.

It is a world of its own, both ancient and contemporary, filled with
seemingly infinite contradictions. Street vendors, bent over and crooked,
cackle across the city pushing carts of vegetables or pastries, while
teenagers with facial piercings and tight clothes saunter by with cell
phones glued to their ears.

Modernity is approaching.
You can almost smell it in the air

Held In The
Heart of Havana

Soft light comes through the slits of the heavy, wooden folding blinds. Dawn kisses my forehead softly. A rooster crows. A child cries in the distance. A surge of delicate wispy bliss pulses through me remembering where I am. This is the morning soundscape of a village awakening. A cacophony of roosters, barking dogs, laughing and crying children, blended with the crescendo of rhythmical incantations of the approaching street vendors creates a musicality unlike any other. I lay motionless next to my lover, listening to the orchestra of life unfolding within me and around me. I am more at peace than I can ever remember being. I feel at home, safe, quiet inside, and filled with love.

I love the way his sculpted body feels next to me. I sink into the rhythm of his breath. He looks like a God sprawled out next to me. Every muscle is so perfectly defined. His square, chiseled jaw and perfect hands and feet are like eye candy to me. I love the stark contrast of the colors of our skin on the white sheets. My desire for him stirs gently as I curl in deeper to him. For three months, we have been planning this trip to be together here for ten days in Cuba. Being here now is the sanctuary we have both been wanting and needing together.

Cuba offers a time away from time, a place away from our mundane worlds of responsibilities, and working too hard to pay bills that never stop coming. It offers us an opportunity to share a world we both love, where humanity is fully acceptable in all of its forms. I wish I could stay here like this next to him all day just absorbing the sounds and smells in tranquility together. I hear his sister shuffling in the kitchen and start to rise. Carlos puts his arm on top of me to keep me from getting up and pulls me back into the bed. We stay in bed together for what feels like a long time, talking, laughing and cherishing these waking moments together before I go to Havana and he gets busy with family affairs.

Hours later, Alexander, the brother of a Cuban friend of mine from Miami, arrives to take me to see some rooms in Havana. Alexander is dressed head to toe in white, with a thick gold chain draping around his neck. He sports a single gold tooth and most definitely, the biggest lips I have ever seen. I can not help but to think he would be the perfect model for a cartoon character with those lips. I have a hard time not staring at them when he talks.

I am pretty sure that he speaks at least one thousand words a minute, none of which I can understand. It sounds like one big word to me, it is so fast. Still somehow, I get the gist enough to understand that the ex-wife of a friend of his has a room he thinks would be suitable for me, at a decent price, and that he would like to show it to me.

Something about his energy and the way he talks and moves makes me feel uncomfortable, on edge and protective. I cannot figure out what it is exactly about him, but I do not feel safe with him. I am grateful when Carlos offers to drive me to Havana to be sure I am safe and settled before he leaves to visit the rest of his family. Obviously Carlos is not getting the best vibe off of Alexander either. I sense that Carlos is also perhaps a little jealous and being protective, which in this instance, I am actually grateful for.

Driving into Havana I feel a mixture of emotions. Moments of *"What am I doing here?"* are followed by feelings of total excitement. As we enter the maze of tight streets that is Havana Vieja, Carlos turns up the volume on the car stereo. I feel like I am in a Cuban reggaeton video, next to a super hot Cuban dressed in pure white, with mirrored shades. We are rolling through Havana like gangsters in gold chains, but without gold chains. As the melodramatic visual play of Havana begins to imprint itself on my mind, I welcome the comic relief of Alexander's huge cartoon character lips flapping in the back seat giving us directions.

The city unfolds through the car window in a flurry of faces, smells, and sounds. The men look directly into my eyes. It feels as if they can see right through me. They meet my eyes fearlessly with an intense, animalistic, sexual hunger that both scares me and excites me at the same time. The women rarely meet my gaze.

Undeniably, Havana has a unique odor. It smells of organic decay and diesel fuel. Somehow, for me, it only adds to the charm rather than detracting from it. It never seems overpowering, but more like a backdrop to some of the inner streets of the city that keeps your senses alive. We cruise slowly into the heart of Central Havana on skinny cobblestone streets packed with bike taxis, food vendors and pedestrians. The music blasting from the windows of the car goes unnoticed by those we pass. This is Cuba after all.

Havana is a city of total contrast everywhere I look. One corner boasts majestic proud buildings of near museum quality. On the next, I see decaying piles of rubble. We are driving deep into the heart of Central Havana. The energy is intense, but light at the same time. Children are playing soccer in the streets barefooted. Piles of overflowing trash are waiting to be picked up by the truck that is cruising behind us. The garbage men, who are bare-chested, skinny men, call out playfully to the children as they toss bags of refuse into the back of the trash truck. My anxiety of the unknown suddenly rises. I notice that I feel edgy, and a little bit afraid of being left here alone with Mr. Big Lips as my guide. I have not even seen the place he wants to show me, but I already know I will not be staying there.

I am every emotion possible. On top of it, I am mentally stretched by trying to speak and understand lightning fast Cuban Spanish. I find myself slapping my hand against the side of the car in rhythm to the music to keep myself grounded. I feel the edges of doubt creeping in about everything I am here to do. Can I really survive in a city this large for a month? It feels intimidating, scary, and like the buildings could just collapse on me at any time. I have never been much of a city girl after all. I grew up in a small town, and I will likely always be a small-town girl at heart.

I suddenly remember reading stories about buildings collapsing here in the city from old age sometimes burying people alive. I ask Carlos and Alexander about it. The answer I get is not reassuring.

"Si, si, it happens," Mr. Big Lips responds.

"One just collapsed close to here last week, but do not worry. The house I am taking you to is two blocks away. It is totally safe."

I find myself wondering how two blocks in this neighborhood could make any difference whatsoever.

We turn another corner and I feel an increasing anxiety as Carlos translates Alexander's words for me while we pull up to the house. I go through the motions of seeing the house he refers me to, and thank Alexander for his help. We stop at a local bar, and I buy him a beer. I tell him I will call him later after lunch. I politely send him on his way, knowing intuitively that Carlos feels the same as I do and that we will find a more suitable accommodation for me, together.

After an hour or so of driving me to look at different places in Havana, I end up choosing a place that came recommended by someone I trust from home. Carlos carries my bags up the three flights of stairs and settles me in before he heads off to see his family.

"Be careful here. I care about you. I do not want anything bad to happen to you. I'll look for you in a few days," he says before he leaves. I am touched by his sincerity. He kisses me quickly and departs.

My new home, for now, is a small room in Havana Vieja. It feels very safe, with a fun lively couple and their little girl. Being with a family feels comforting to me. I am pleased that it is also very clean and incredibly quiet for being in the heart of a city of over two million people. I realize that these old buildings create an effective sound barrier. Peace can be found even in the midst of the chaos of the city outside.

I am completely exhausted by 8 pm. I do not feel ready to take on anything else. Alone at last in my room I am content. My wild side wants to go out and wander Havana, to dance all night and rock it. My wise side reminds me that I have three weeks ahead of me and that rest and some quiet time are what's needed right now on my first night alone in Havana. It is hard to resist the sounds of drums bouncing off the walls into my window, but I dig out my ear plugs and in minutes I am fast asleep. I feel held and safe in the heart of Havana.

Morning Meanderings

The sweat pours off my face. I can taste the salt in the air and in my sweat. Everything around me smells of life and death at the same time. Wafts of rotting fish chunks that fishermen used as bait greet me, left on the concrete from the night before. The scent of fresh ground coffee, and petrol fumes mix in the air around me as I stroll along the Malecón. The smell is far from displeasing; it is instead a pungent reminder that life is happening all around me.

The Malecón is famous in Havana. It is a broad esplanade, roadway, and seawall that stretches for five miles along the coast in Havana. Construction was started by the Americans in 1901 to protect Havana from the sea, and completed by Cuba in 1923. It now runs from the mouth of the harbor in Old Havana (Havana Vieja), along the north side of the Centro Habana neighborhood and the Vedado neighborhood, and ends at the mouth of the Almendares River. You can see the outline of the city from here. It is the perfect place to gaze across the harbor and dream. It is a favorite spot for Cubans, and travelers alike with its beautiful vistas of the city and the ocean. It grants serenity from the bustling activity of the city streets. At night, the Malecón comes alive with performers, fishermen and the youth who hang out all night long beneath the stars talking, laughing, drinking rum and playing music.

Sitting with my back to the water, enjoying the sight of the city sprawling out in front of me, my eyes feast on beautifully restored colonial buildings as they hover over ghetto-like, barely-standing hovels of decay. Wrinkled and aged Cuban women shuffle by me in clothing that looks like it soon may be made into rags. Across the street, men smoking cigars sit in doorways watch the city roll by quietly, as puffs of smoke float up from their cracked lips. I cannot help but wonder what their lives have been like. They offer a smile and "good day" to me.

I sit by the water and watch the city wake up, breathing in the smells and sights of Havana until the sun is burning my skin. It is hot today, and while I don't mind the sweat, the sun gets the best of me. I stroll casually back to my casa as if I know where I am going. I do not. I have no idea where I am or where my casa is from where I sat by the water. I just arrived in Havana, and I don't know it very well yet. I just got lucky ending up here along the water this morning in my meanderings. I let the process of being lost become a practice in faith. The journey of discovery is beginning. Wandering aimlessly through this maze of concrete and humanity offers me windows into daily life for Cubans in Havana. Sounds, sights, smells, they all become a rich tapestry for contemplation and exploration.

This city writhes with sexual desire, lust and passion. There is an intoxicating animalistic pulse that permeates the air here, all day and all night. It's almost palpable. The heat seems to intensify it. Life feels juicy, sensual, stimulating and passionate somehow. The men here seem always ready to devour anything in their path with their lustful eyes. The younger women display their receptivity non-stop with their revealing skin tight clothes, sassy swishing hips and perfectly parted lips. The sensuality of life lingers on every corner and adds to the richness of Havana's street life.

There is absolutely nothing prudish about Cuba. The women are comfortable dressing provocatively at almost any age. The men are not shy at all about expressing their sexual desires and appreciation for a woman's beauty. Yet, interestingly, it never feels overdone or inappropriate as it might back home. I noticed the same thing last time I was in Cuba, a few years ago. Sexuality and sensuality are so natural here. People's connection to their sexuality is not based on trying to look perfect. It is organic, and relaxed. This is refreshing coming from the USA where women are getting boob jobs and botox at increasingly younger ages, trying to conform to ridiculous ideals of beauty. I love that here, women of all shapes and sizes are considered sexy. I love that larger, voluptuous women flaunt their curves just as shamelessly as skinny, smaller women. I love that they are so accepting of all kinds of beauty in every form. I love that the men don't seem to have filters for some ideal perfect form to appreciate a woman's beauty.

Cubans are known to be quite open with their sexuality and sensuality. Men and women alike are often promiscuous, playful and provocative in mannerisms and socialization. Most of it is very innocent and just the way the people are with each other naturally. Perhaps due to the illegalization of pornography, sexuality in Cuba is more freely expressed, not hidden. Their connection to sexuality is very healthy. When people talk about Cuba being "hot" they mean more than the temperature of the air. It's a sexy culture and a sexy place all the way through. The refreshing part of it for me is that being sexy or hot has absolutely nothing to do with having a perfect body. Cubans see beyond the form to the inside. They look deeper than the surface when they look at you. In a moment they can read your inner world and sense your energy. It is that poignancy of perception and the way that the people can see right to your soul that makes Cuba ooze with sensual sexuality.

As I walk through the streets, I find myself passing through the Plaza de Armas and onto Calle Obispo, which is one of the main commercial and tourist streets of Havana. Plaza de Armas is already awake and alive. Many of the park benches that frame the plaza are filled with Cubans chatting. A group of street performers are preparing for their first pass of the day in their bright-colored costumes with tassels, whistles and drums strung around their bodies. Their laughter and high energy chatter brings a smile to my heart. Plaza de Armas is the oldest of Havana's infamous squares dating back to the early 1520s. Originally, it was known as the Plaza de Iglesia after a church that once stood where the present-day Palacio de los Capitanes Generales sits. The name was changed to Plaza de Armas in the late 16th century when the governor used the site to conduct military exercises. Today it is a beautiful place to sit and watch the world go by, framed with shade trees, palms and a few cafés where you can enjoy a good Cuban coffee. It is also a historic and touristic center with a marble statue of Carlos Manuel de Céspedes at its center. Céspedes is highly revered in Cuba as a revolutionary who set Cuba on the road to independence in 1868.

Calle Obispo empties right into Plaza de Armas. Obispo leads you deeper into the heart of Havana Vieja. Calle Obispo dates back to 1519, only four years after the founding of Havana. The street was originally created as a very narrow passageway to help provide a shady passage from the center of the city to the Plaza de Armas and the sea beyond the Plaza. Now it is a commercial center filled with public buildings, restaurants, utilities, stores, cafés, bakeries, and even some famous hotels, such as the Hotel Ambos Mundos which became well known as Ernest Hemingway's favorite hangout in Havana.

I visited Havana a few times on my first trip to Cuba. I am a little bit surprised by the changes I am seeing. I knew change would come with the Obama administration's openings for US citizens to travel to Cuba in 2012. Change is inevitable. It is only a matter of time before Cuba will be inundated with cell phones, computers, and internet access. I feel grateful that I got to experience Cuba before technology put its claws deep into this island's thick skin.

Modern culture is definitely finding its way in through the cracks in the crumbling walls of this city. I can see a marked difference here since my last trip to visit Havana.[1] Fancy stores with new modern storefronts, expensive clothes and even a few brand name stores have found a place in Old Havana now. Somehow it saddens me knowing that many will want what very few can afford here. With salaries here still very low, averaging from $10 US a month for a school teacher or social worker, to highs of $50 US per month for a doctor, it is hard to imagine how any Cuban could possibly afford $100 for designer shoes, or $200 for an expensive watch. Clearly, these stores are here to cater to tourists. It will also create an impact in the mind of the

---

1   2012

Cubans who live and work here on what they will strive for. Values will shift and materialism will begin to be more commonplace.

The youth display an ultra-hip, city vibe. Their hunger for what the rest of the world has is clearly revealed in their attire and attitude. So much has changed so fast. It is now common to see young people with tattoos, piercings and cell phones glued to their ears. They are ready, and ripe for change, and understandably so after nearly five decades with little influence or input from the outside world. I learn from people on the streets that some people are getting access to the internet, cable TV and programs from the USA in their homes, illegally of course. I imagine pornography too has found its way in, and the innocence of their sexuality will become like ours, forever polluted. Cubans who live outside are bringing in hard drives and USB drives filled with media, movies, and music from the outside world. Of course tourism also has a big influence on access to information.

Cuban media and website access is tightly controlled. During the past several decades, Cubans have seen very little violence on television. The government does not allow distribution of programs that are excessively violent or sexual on public television. As of now, the internet is only available at hotels on very slow computers for a very high price per hour. Site access is greatly restricted, and there is very little capability for most websites to be viewed or accessed. Blocks are placed on pornography sites, and specific media outlets. Very few Cubans are able to access the internet anyway, and in some places it is completely non-existent.

Apparently, that is beginning to change in Havana. Cubans are masters of ingenuity and solutions to complex problems are always found eventually. Due to the lack of material goods and resources on the island, they have had to learn to be creative, and to make what they have last as long as possible. If something is broken, a Cuban will come up with a creative way to fix it, with bubblegum and shoelaces if necessary. Knowing this about Cubans, it is not surprising to me to learn that they are finding ways to get themselves connected to the internet in spite of the challenges (and illegality) of it in 2012. The underground world of black market providers has always found inroads to bring the Cuban people what they want, and now with wifi and the tech world, they are doing the same. It is being made available to those "inner circle" Cubans who can afford it, at premium prices and with great risks if caught, in spite of the government's regulations.

Havana is clearly already well on its way to full-scale modernization. More access to technology is inevitable. For that I am both happy for what they will gain, and sad for them in what they risk losing. I only pray that Cuba can find ways to learn from our mistakes and not suffer the same kind of disconnection, depression and dysfunctions that we have endured at the hands of the technological revolution.

Visiting Ishmael

Carlos comes for me just after breakfast to drive me to Cojimar to visit my family of friends there. He is sullen and solemn this morning. He does not want to talk. I do not pry. He keeps his hand on my thigh as we ride together quietly out of the center of Havana. We dip down under the tunnel and as we float back out of it, the ocean spreads out into infinity along the highway. We are both lost in our own thoughts, until finally we come to the village of Cojimar.

My first trip to Cuba, I spent the entirety of my time in this dusty little village near the sea. Cojimar spreads out along the shoreline just a short drive from the hustle and bustle of Havana. It was made famous as one of Hemingway's favorite home bases in Cuba. Hemingway spent a great deal of time in Cuba and in particular, in Cojimar, in the 1940s and 1950s. He was well-loved amongst the Cuban people, and he, like myself, loved Cuba dearly. In 1951, reportedly unhappy with the reception given *Across the River and Into the Trees*, Hemingway began writing a short novel drawing on the colorful stories and people he encountered while fishing and drinking in and around Cojimar, where he berthed *Pilar*, his boat.

In 1952 he published what would become a Pulitzer Prize Winner, *The Old Man and the Sea*. There is a large statue of Hemingway near the fort on the coast of Cojimar. If you are in Cojimar long enough and talk to the right old timers, you may just get lucky enough to meet one of his old friends from back in the day. If you meet one, invite them for a coffee or a beer and take time to hear a few of their stories. They will tell you what it was like sharing rum and cigars with the great American novelist before he took his life in 1961.

Hemingway has always been one of my favorite writers. I was an avid reader of his work as a child growing up in Florida. Every year, my family visited the Florida Keys, and I always insisted on visiting his home there and seeing his famous feline friends with eight to ten toes per paw. My mother would take me and we would sit sometimes for hours in the courtyard of Hemingway's home. I always felt close to him somehow. I was a child then, no more than ten or twelve years old, yet I loved his stories. I was an avid reader at a young age. I felt safe and good when we visited his home in Key West. I loved hearing stories about his adventures and I would stare at the photos of him for long periods of time, so inspired by his life and work. The candid, easy way he wrote his stories were some of the first moments that made me want to become a writer as a child. When I unexpectedly ended up along the same path as Hemingway in Cuba, I knew that I wanted to share my story. I knew that I wanted my first book to be starting in this place so that I could leave some part of my legacy in the same place that one of my great inspirations left his.

Nearing Cojimar now, my heart is doing backflips. I am so excited to see my friends again. After so long of not being able to see them or communicate with them, I am just praying everyone is healthy and home. Phone calls to and from Cuba are very expensive, nearly $1/minute. Calls almost always drop. Often it's nearly impossible to get through. None of my friends in Cojimar have cell phones. The cell phones that are available in Cuba right now are mostly the old style flip phones. Data plans for internet access on the cell phone have yet to become available in Cuba, so there is no Facebook, IM, or texting access for them yet. It will come, all too soon. As much as I want them to be able to communicate, I also know that when cell phones and data plans do enter Cuba, it will forever change the culture, just as it has changed ours in the world outside of Cuba. For these reasons, I have had very little contact with my friends since I left Cuba. I hope they are all here and well. I feel a little anxious excitement brewing as we turn down the broken roads towards Ishmael's home.

I navigate as Carlos drives, until we pull up to the white pillars outside of Ishmael's home. He has no idea I am back on the island, so this will be a big surprise for him. We honk the horn once in front of his gate and I step out of the car and go to the door and call his name.

"Oye, Ishmael? Dónde estas hermano mio?" I call out, my Spanish is only slightly better than it was when we first met.

Ishmael comes rolling out with a huge smile on his face. When I visited Cuba the first time, this gentle giant of a man became like a father and brother to me. Ishmael was that gentle, but strong masculine presence that a man should be: protective but never overbearing. He was always deeply respectful to me, and also to every woman I saw him interact with, in a fatherly/brotherly manner. He was always caring and always inquiring into my life out of genuine interest. He was my teacher, my friend, and my rock of stability, as well as my place of safe refuge when I landed in Cuba the first time. Men like Ishmael are rare in almost every culture and appreciated by all who get to know them, both men and women alike. A man who has respect, dignity and pride in being a gentleman, is one to be admired. In the three weeks I was in Cojimar before, I spent more time with Ishmael than anyone else. Most definitely, he is the person I have missed the most. He helped me to heal so many parts of my heart. He never asked me for anything, but always wanted to give, nurture, protect and serve in any way he could. He is a classic Cuban gentleman instilled with the old school values of the culture in every fiber of his being.

We are both so happy to see each other again. Tears flow from our eyes and hearts as we embrace. We look at each other, amazed that we are standing in front of each other again. His laughter lights up my world.

Jesuscito, my drum teacher, is on the roof of the house next door and hollers down to me with a huge smile on his face. "Oye, Cheri! Espereme!" Carlos is standing next to the car watching me greet my friends. I know he has to get on his way to go see his extended family. I quickly introduce him to Ishmael then accompany him back to the car to see him off.

"You are sure you are OK here alone?" He says to me, obviously a little concerned. I sense a hint of jealousy, but I brush it off in my joy of reunion with my friends and teachers.

"Yes, yes. This is family. I am so safe here. I will get a taxi back later, do not worry. Go and enjoy your family. I'll see you when you get back." I give him a quick kiss and watch him drive away.

Ishmael and Jesuscito stand together inside of the gate, both in total surprise. They are laughing together, joyful and excited. They had no idea I was coming for a visit. I had tried several times to phone Ishmael, but was never able to get through, so I decided to take a chance and just show up. I felt sure they would both be around first thing in the morning. Ishmael is scurrying around, trying to clean up and make a space for me to sit down inside. Jesuscito is smiling as he lights a cigarette repeating my name and mumbling something to himself happily.

The familial love between the three of us is so pure, just as it always was. My mind wanders back to so many memories shared with these two precious souls. We spent hours and days together sitting behind the house playing drums, singing, talking, sharing, laughing and trying to understand each other with my pathetic Spanish. I came here every day for lessons, or sometimes to prepare together before going to a Santería Ceremony in a nearby village. Ishmael's house was the focal point of my first experience in Cuba, and as such it feels like a homecoming just being here with the two of them again.

I have to catch my breath when I enter Ishmael's house. The strong smell of animal manure permeates the air from the pigs and chickens he raises for money. I do not remember his house looking this bad when I was here before. I wonder if he has been sick or depressed lately and just not been able to maintain things, or if he has had more financial difficulty and not able to afford to fix things.

Jesuscito looks older, more worn, and tired. His hair has gone completely gray and he is much thinner, and gaunt. He was always very skinny anyway, but now it seems much more so. He does not look well. I put my hand on his shoulder, and looked into his eyes.

"Jesus, estás bien?" I ask him.

"Si, si, todo bien," but he looks away towards the floor as he says it. His eyes do not meet mine. I send a silent blessing to my beloved teacher and friend knowing he is suffering and does not want to burden me with it. He always had a hard time eating. He was very thin before, but now he looks almost emaciated. He has aged considerably. I am sure it is the rum.

Ishmael comes towering out, all smiles and pure love pouring out of him. He embraces me, chattering away a mile a minute with enthusiasm. He leads me to the porch to sit and talk. He is so excited that I am here. The innocence of his love strikes me as almost childlike. The three of us sit together on the porch and share, catching up on life together. When Jesuscito leaves to go next door I ask Ishmael about his health. He confirms for me that Jesuscito has been very sick, his liver and gallbladder damaged by the years of rum, coffee and cigarettes.

"Él no quiere comer nada, siempre flaco pero ahora, demasiado," (He doesn't want to eat anything. He's always been skinny, but now it's too much) Ishmael says. He quickly changes the subject, and with Jesuscito reapproaching, I leave it alone and let the conversation move on. They fill me in on my other friends there. We decide to take a stroll together to visit some of the neighbors so that I may pay my respects. As we saunter through the village, everyone greets me with big hugs and so much love it is almost overwhelming. It is truly a homecoming for my heart.

After visiting with everyone, Ishmael and I walk to the market together, arm in arm. I buy a big bag of vegetables and food for us, knowing he probably has not had fresh vegetables in some time. Being with him again is incredibly comforting: a reminder of how timeless true friendship is. We walk back to his house laughing and chatting like no time has passed at all.

I make him a salad with fried green tomatoes, doing my best to work in his kitchen that is deeply in need of cleaning. The smell of the animals from the back courtyard permeates the kitchen through the open windows. I put my mind to the task of making a healthy meal for us in an obviously unsanitary environment. Inwardly, I bless the food, and pray that I do not get sick.

I'm concerned about his home. It looks to be literally falling apart. The cracks in the wall have gotten bigger, the paint is falling off even more, the metal and wood makeshift chairs are barely held together. I can hear water running in the bathroom. I ask him about it. He shows me that his shower head fixture has broken and laughing, he tells me it costs 50 CUC to fix so he lives with it like this. Obviously, he does not have 50 CUC, but I do. I give it to him without hesitation. He hugs me with tears in his eyes.

We spend a few more hours together, and in what feels like a short breath it is almost sunset and time for me to go back to Havana. Ishmael makes a phone call and arranges a private ride back to the city for me for 5 CUC, which is much less than I would have gotten on my own. I can remember being asked for up to 20 CUC for this same ride in the past. As I walk back to my casa, from the taxi along the Malecón, I reflect on the incredible contradictions that exist in this culture.

The taxi system is perhaps one of the most perplexing things to understand. There are tourist taxis, and there are Cuban taxis, referred often to as *macinas*. The price for a ride in a taxi can range from 20 cents to twenty, thirty or even fifty dollars, for the same route depending on the day, the time of day, the kind of car, the driver, the knowledge of the passenger, and the nationality of the passenger. The Cubans themselves, when asked to explain the disparity, shake their heads in confusion.

For example: a ride from the airport to a casa or hotel in Havana Vieja is typically 20-25 CUC for a tourist taxi.[2] However, depending on a variety of factors, that price can be per person, or per car. The airport to Havana Vieja is about 25-30 minutes on a good day without too much traffic. For about that same price, per person, in a *taxi colectivo*, or shared taxi, you can go from Havana, door to door, to Trinidad or Cienfuegos which are three to four hours away in a

---

2   2012

good, strong modern car. If it is late at night, you might be asked for that amount to go from a bar near the Malecón, to your casa in Havana Vieja or from Havana Vieja to Vedado which is a ten to fifteen minute ride maximum.

Around town in Havana can be even more confusing until one learns the systems, the language, and how to navigate the routes and options around the city. The *macinas* that the Cubans use for their transport are typically paid in Cuban Pesos or National Money (CUP).[3] An unknowing foreigner may easily pay in Cuban Convertible Pesos or CUC and still think he is getting a bargain compared to the tourist taxis which usually are more on demand and can be door to door services. The *macinas* have specific routes and can range from 5 CUP (Cuban Pesos) up to 50 CUP if it is a longer ride, or if it is late at night, or a Sunday, or if the driver just happens to feel like asking you for more.

For the exact same distance and the exact same route, with maybe a few less blocks to walk, and no stops to pick up other passengers, the tourist taxis will charge 10-20 CUC. Using the easiest calculation of approximately 25 CUP to 1 CUC, when you do the math you can easily understand how the tourist taxis can be taking in hundreds of dollars a day.

However, this is Cuba, so while they may get lucky enough on occasion to take in hundreds a day, that does not mean they are profiting as much as one might think. Most of the drivers have to pay the state or a private owner to use the car. You might consider it something like a per day rental cost. I have had drivers tell me they pay anywhere from $25-$100 a day for using the cars, again depending on many factors including the kind of car, who they are renting it from, who their clients will be, and what kind of use they are anticipating, etc. In addition, they also must pay a percentage of what they earned to the state, and of course there are hard costs

---

3   In The Breath of Cuba Part I, I go into depth on the monetary system. In short 1 CUC is the equivalent of 24-25 CUP. Cubans are paid typically in CUP but most household goods and many foods are sold in CUC making it very difficult for the average Cuban to purchase.

like petrol, and/or unexpected maintenance costs that have to be figured in. Getting a tire fixed may not seem like a big deal to an American, but to a Cuban it can be a very costly and sometimes nearly impossible endeavor that can take hours or days to remedy. The taxis are one small example of a system that is inexplicable and baffles my mind if I try to assume anything is logical here whatsoever.

The moon comes up slowly, shimmering across the sea. I pause to sit on the seawall to enjoy the moonrise. I am so content to be back on this rock, feeling the pulse and rhythm of this beautiful strange island I have fallen head over heels in love with. I feel content being alone tonight, cherishing the time with my thoughts to reflect on my journey so far. Going to Cojimar to see my friends today was healing and therapeutic.

Thus far, I have spent my nights in Havana walking endlessly in search of that deep intimacy that I came to know in the living rooms and back porches in Cojimar. More often, I find a disco with reggaeton or an over glamorized tourist scene with pasty, plump whiteys who just took their first salsa class in the hotel lobby.

In comparison to what I experienced in the pueblo of Cojimar during my last trip, Havana feels to me a lot like a Cuban sandwich in Cuba: mostly bread with a wispy thin, barely visible piece of meat inside. Overpriced for its nutritional content, it may fill you up but it may leave you hungry for something more.

There is no doubt in my mind now, after a short visit to Cojimar, that I am looking in the wrong place for the kind of community of music and dance that I want to experience. The city is not for me. Havana is fun for a few days. I do love the beauty and architecture, the history and art and the vibe of Havana. Yet, for a longer stay, I find myself craving the quiet serenity of village life. I miss the sounds of the roosters in the mornings and the soft sounds of the day unfolding. I enjoy cities in small doses. Cities are cities. Each has its own unique character, but all fall short of the intimacy I crave that a smaller town or village inherently inspires. Get in and get out has always been my city philosophy and Havana, even with all its magic and beauty, is not the place I want to be for much longer.

I find myself wondering about my intentions for this trip to immerse myself more in the Cuban culture, music and dancing. I feel a fear of failure surfacing. As I stroll past a little old toothless lady dressed in a ridiculously frivolous red dress with a weird-looking shaved dog in her lap waving at me joyfully, I find myself laughing at my own western neurosis of thinking too much.

There is nothing to fail at. Life is to live, not only to achieve. I remind myself that I have to accept the reality that intentions and plans aside, the journey will reveal itself to me in its own time. What I think I am here for, and what I am really here for, may indeed be different realities. I have to be open to what is present rather than stuck on my agenda. I remind myself that everything is perfect just the way it is. If I do nothing at all, and achieve nothing at all, that too is perfect.

After all, I am in Cuba, and Cuba will have its own agenda for me. I choose to stop striving, enjoy being, and let the moments unfold.

Peace returns and I feel alive and content as Oya wraps her breath around me once again.

The Two Faces of Cuba

People here wear two faces.
One is tired, worn and hopeless, with a furrowed brow
that is lined by a learned acceptance of the futility of life in a world
that never seems to change or offer them more than crumbs.

The other is friendly, tender and always welcoming, ready to stop,
dance and enjoy the music the moment the beat drops
to celebrate life in any moment, for any reason.

I am filled today with an inexplicable sadness. Maybe something of the despair of this city has gotten into me. Maybe I am just tired. Maybe it is both. I find myself looking deeply into the eyes of the old people I pass on the street to feel what they might feel. I enter their eyes and it is as if I can almost see through their window of hopelessness. I walk the streets today allowing myself to experience what it might feel like to live in one of these crumbling alleyway apartments. I try to let myself feel what it would be like to live here, with rats scurrying across the floor, buildings randomly collapsing, and strong pungent smells always in the ethers from all directions. What would it be like knowing that this is all I will ever have; all I will ever get to know or experience. Sinking into that reality, and imagining what may go on behind the vacant stares I see today, the sadness in me knows no end.

There is no way out. This is it, and nothing more can ever be. I do not have any opportunity for anything different. Even if I work every day, in a full time job, it is impossible to make enough money to improve my situation. Fresh fruits or vegetables, quality clothes, fixing my home or having money to purchase commodities are all out of my scope financially. Even if I could afford to travel, which of course I can not, I am not permitted to travel to another province to look for a better life, without the threat of being arrested or returned. There is no change coming here, not in my lifetime. Nothing will ever be any different from how it is now. My whole existence is simply to try to survive another day. My only ray of light, my only joy, is to find some comfort in sharing the day with a family member or friend who understands my reality as their own.

It is an intense and surreal practice for me to contemplate what lives are like. The eyes that are looking into mine are incredible windows. As I wander off the beaten track, I see into a reality that is tucked away and hidden from the tourists in this vast concrete jungle of Havana.

I walk slowly, with no destination. I am intentionally taking the streets that feel the least travelled by the white-skinned camera carriers. I let myself spend several hours in this way, witnessing the reality of Havana's inner world behind the carefully crafted facade of tourist attractions. Decrepit buildings, trash-strewn streets, shoeless children and mangy dogs speckle my vision. I see the lame ones, with lifeless limbs hanging from ragged, dirty clothes. I look into the eyes of the diseased with bumps and lesions all over their skin, and wonder if there is a cure for them. I marvel that in a country that boasts free medical care for all, with highly skilled doctors, there are so many who seem to be suffering without care.

My heart breaks open a hundred times a minute. Compassion comes flooding in. I offer greetings to the hunched over elders, who smile back at me with toothless grins even in their pain and suffering. I purposely get lost in their maze. I am alone in my world of experiencing a part of this place that most would intentionally avoid. Yet, even in these parts, I saw the community and their love in motion. I received warmhearted smiles from strangers. Never did I feel unsafe, not for a moment. I saw them taking the time to stop and chat, calling out to each other in the streets with loud, strong voices. I witnessed a proud, connected people in spite of their differences and difficulties. What impressed me the most was the simple acknowledgment of humanity. All of them humbly sharing in a reality that, in my culture, would be considered inhumane and impoverished. Ironically, humanity is very alive and there is an abundance of love and spirit that the wealthy in my country lack with all their material wealth and perfectly manicured homes and nails.

People here wear two faces. One is tired, worn and hopeless, with a deep furrowed brow, lined by a learned acceptance of the futility of life in a world that never seems to change or offer them more than crumbs. It is the face of exhaustion, repressed anger, depression, and despair.

The other is smiling, friendly, tender and always welcoming, ready to stop, dance and enjoy the music the moment the beat drops to celebrate life in any moment, for any reason. This is the face of the Cuban who has found the ability to not let the incredible weight of a despairing life destroy his spirit or rob her of the zest for life.

Walking the streets of Havana these past few days, I have seen so much of both. Here lives an undeniable sense of hopelessness, matched with a spirit of acceptance for what is. That acceptance is then gracefully framed with an innate ability to embrace life fully with no expectations or assumptions that life should be any different from what it is. This ability allows the people here to find some sense of peace and enjoy their lives in spite of their circumstances and struggles.

My culture could learn so much from the Cubans' ability to adapt and embrace reality fully. We spend so much of our time and money resisting reality, or worse, trying to change reality into something we can control. The American way has always been about progress at any and all expense: more, faster, better, and never ever stop striving for more, faster, better. In that vein, we have created a neurosis. That neurosis leaves us empty inside. We can never truly relax and enjoy what is, before we are pushing on to try to get to the next best thing, the next best relationship, the next best job, the bigger house, the newer car, the most updated phone, more money and on and on. As a result, many Americans live with constant dissatisfaction with the mundane, boring normalcy that is life itself. Our expectations of life are much like the stuff Disney is made of: happily ever after, the perfect American Dream life, with the white picket fence, the trophy spouse and basically, layer upon layer of illusion. No wonder depression and mental illness are on the rise in our country. When people are forced to come to terms with the reality of life, most of them are not prepared or willing to accept that life isn't actually always happy endings and steamy romances. It is not surprising that so many elders become bitter after being sold a whole world of fairy tales about how perfect life should have been for them if they worked hard, saved their money and had a good retirement plan.

In Havana, however, in spite of old, falling down homes, rags for clothes, and barely enough food to eat, they still make time to enjoy each other. Most importantly, they have not lost their ability to smile and celebrate life. In spite of the incredible stench of piss and filthy streets that they have to navigate every day, they smile. In spite of the knowingness that it is unlikely that anything will ever change for them in their lifetime, they smile. In spite of the fact that their government has effectively made them prisoners on this island, with life sentences to live forever this way, they laugh. Their humanity is intact and they still enjoy spontaneous moments of song and dance with total freedom and joy. Those of us from the modern world could learn a lot from them about how to live in joy, in spite of the imminent suffering that life can be.

The contradictions here are difficult, if not impossible, for a foreigner to understand. The Cuban system, culture, and thought process is so vastly different from what I am accustomed to in the USA. The laws, the mindset and the ideology here are often very hard for me to fully grasp. I am sure I will never truly understand it all. Politics has influenced psychology and culture in profound and mysterious ways. This has in turn influenced the very fabric of life itself in Cuba.

Cuba is a fascinating experiment in humanity and socialization. It has no parallels in the modern world. The idealism behind this social experiment, in its philosophical sense, is noble and beautiful in many ways, and equally insidious and evil in others. Similar to all political ideologies, idealism and reality are worlds apart. What I see is that there seems to be more invested in preserving a very particular balance of life, than granting individual freedoms and rights to the people. In other words, personal liberties, or the rights of a human being as an individual are less important here than the rights of the greater population or community.

It is a concept that is generally foreign to Americans, and something we are inherently opposed to. For the most part, the average US citizen would consider their personal liberties and rights to be far more important than those of the greater communities we live in. The right for individuals to bear arms is more important than the right for the entire community to live without the threat of ever being shot at. The right to profits today is more important than the value of our natural world's preservation for us, and our children's children tomorrow. The right of each individual to express themselves freely is more important than the damage that expression might be able to do to society or other individuals.

In Cuba, as a rule, it seems to me that individual liberties are simply considered less important than the needs of the greater community. The people do not think of and for just themselves as individuals the way we often do in the USA. In contrast to the American culture, not everything here is about individual profit and gain. The focus here is often more about preserving the balance of life, simple safety and survival for all. The needs of the family matters more than the needs of each individual in the household.

It is almost as if there is no "I" but always and only a "we" to consider. It is a different way of thinking and being. I believe that this arises not just from the ideology and politics of socialism or communism, but that it is also an inherent attribute of African indigenous tribal cultures.

The African roots of Cuba shine through in the way the community functions in all parts of Cuba, including Havana. We hear it in the rhythm and the music. We feel it in the dance and in the open-hearted sensual playfulness that Cuba is famous for. We can see the influence of the Afro roots almost everywhere, especially when you look into the way Cubans function and adapt inside of the system of socialism that exists today.

African culture has, at its core, a deep understanding of the need to preserve human life, and of the natural balance of ecosystems for survival. In tribal cultures, it is the norm that individual needs are willingly sacrificed to ensure the safety and protection of the tribe. Everything is shared. Those who act in ways that are for their own selfish gains are often ostracized and sometimes even killed for such behaviors. The African slaves that were brought to Cuba instilled this way of thinking into the very fabric of survival and life in Cuba. Long before Castro, socialism or communism arrived in Cuba, the roots of many of these philosophies and ideas came firmly rooted in the minds, hearts, DNA and cultural conditioning of the Africans who were forced into slavery. The Spanish ideals, and the American influences that came much later to Cuba's soil, all added to the way the culture has evolved over the years. With the dominant African population that Cuba still has, many of the cultural norms of Africa are still very alive. Cuba also had influences from France and Italy, as well as the Moors, the Chinese, and of course, Russia.

The thing that fascinates me the most about Cuba is this diverse mix of cultures that made Cuba, Cuba. When I think about how the African tribal cultures mixed with the Spanish, European, and indigenous cultures, I can see how many people in Cuba today still align with the ideals that Castro's vision of Cuba was originally founded on. Castro's original idealistic vision gave validity to a deep cultural norm that still thrives in many of the villages and cities of Africa and Cuba today. Sharing, equality, health care and education for all, and a sovereign nation were all very attractive ideals to a nation that was under the heavy hand of the American-placed dictator, Batista. It is a fact that it seems few people acknowledge or discuss, but Cuba was under a brutal dictator long before Castro. Batista was no angel. He was being handsomely paid to allow Cuba to be overrun by Italian Mafia, and American interests. The CIA reported that during Batista's reign, over twenty thousand people were murdered by the police or the Cuban Rural Guard. Most were tortured in the most horrible ways a human being could imagine, horrifically murdered, then displayed publicly to create fear of retribution amongst the Cubans. On many occasions, these murders were categorized as "massacres" because it wasn't only one person to be killed. It was reported that at times, Batista's police would block of the exits to a city block and murder the entire community in that street systematically, and sometimes drag the corpses through the streets to be publicly seen. The actual number of Cubans killed under Batista will never be known as it is estimated that thousands of these cases were never reported nor documented. On many occasions, the blacks were gathered up and killed en masse in the streets of Havana and Santiago. Many people were not happy under Batista either. Prostitution, gang violence, drugs and all the sicknesses of modern culture were becoming firmly rooted in Cuba under his regime. Castro's message spoke to the heart of the Cuban people, and their rich cultural heritage. He offered the people hope and change by returning the land to the Cuban people and taking care of everyone equally. He promised every Cuban a home, education, health care and basics for food and survival.

How could they have known then that they would be trading one brutal dictatorship for another? (The CIA reports that Castro's reign was responsible for nearly fourteen thousand political killings in comparison to Batista's twenty thousand plus)

Yet still, many Cubans I have met in my journeys tell me that they feel Castro did more for Cuba's sovereignty than any other leader and they are still devoted to the Revolution's cause. Many of the elders in Cuba still have fond memories of the Revolution, and in general in Cuba, it is more common to hear people speak of Castro with respect for his higher idealism than one might imagine.

Of course, in reality, in today's Cuba, this precarious balance the government is trying to hold the country in, is not necessarily one that all of the people want preserved. Many have suffered for too long. Like all political systems, there are many aspects that are not in service to the people's best interest. Idealism vs reality never seems to be a match in any system. Many Cubans lost everything they had during Castro's Revolution, and they are understandably traumatized, angry and resentful. Other Cubans gained access to things they could never have had without the Revolution. The lack of resources and provisions have created very real and unique challenges in Cuba, most of which no foreigner could ever have any ability to truly understand, even by living amongst Cubans for many years.

Darlene, the Cuban woman that owns the casa particular where I have been staying, explained it to me on a long walk through the streets of Havana under the guise of looking for someplace to dance salsa. We never found the dance, instead we ended up just strolling casually for hours, happily chatting. She is one of the few Cubans I have met in Havana who speaks a little English. I enjoy hearing her perspectives very much.

"Cheri: Mira (look), here in Cuba, we no pay for nothing like you do. My house, I no pay rent. If I get sick, I no pay Doctor. Liposuction, I want to get. Free for me. I no pay much for electricity, or water. Food is very cheap and some of it free. My sister, she live in Hialeah. She tell me people shoot children in the street and she no like leave house anymore. She scared of everyone there. Many crazy people in your country no? Many people have guns? I hear children are killing children? What is wrong with your country? You understand me? In your country, you pay a lot of money just for rent no? Doctor is very expensive. You no money, you no house. You no money, you no have food. For you, is very hard. Me, I prefer Cuba."

In spite of all the problems, and there are plenty of them, I have heard scores of Cubans share this perspective with me. They have a certain (albeit low level) security of at least having some of their basic needs provided for them. They know also that if they don't have enough, their family or their neighbors will help them, without a doubt. When I walk these streets all day and all night absorbing the energy, I begin to understand this one thing to be the source of the general feeling of peacefulness that presides here.

For the most part, in talking to the Cubans I have met, it appears that the people mostly get along pretty well with each other. They are willing to share. They willingly and joyfully help each other out with just about anything at just about any time of the day or night. They have to be this way to survive, it is true. Yet, there is a quality of sincerity beneath it that I rarely see anymore in my own country. They seem to truly enjoy each other and they get satisfaction out of helping each other any way they can. They value their time together as friends and family. They are always thinking creatively to survive and this keeps them mentally fit. They are masters of finding ways around the system to get their needs met.

In contemplating some of the laws and prohibitions here in Cuba, the argument could be made that there may have originally been a sincere intention to protect the entire population at the expense of individual rights. Some things that are prohibited here are allowed in the USA under the concept of "freedom of expression." I am not at all 100 percent convinced that it has served us much better than the restraints on this have served Cuba. We have lost a lot of our innocence and personal safety in the things we have been exposed to. This, possibly could be correlated to the freedoms granted to psychologically sick minds under this right of freedom of expression.

In the states, we glorify violence and accept pornography as normal parts of our culture. In Cuba, there are tight controls placed on these things. That control has resulted in a population that still has a certain respect and purity of spirit that is actually quite natural outside of modern culture's insidious impacts on human psychology. They have not lost their innocence, not yet. Sadly, with the approach of modern technology, soon they too will be exposed to the depths of the dark side of what too much uncensored freedom of expression can create in the human psyche.

Of course, as with most things in government and systems of control, either option can be taken too far. My western Americanized mind defaults often to the argument of "personal responsibility and independence." What Darlene shared with me, in essence, was that she feels her government basically is trying to protect her more than control her. If I were to paraphrase what she seemed to be expressing it would be more or less the following:

"One individual's poor personal judgement, psychological imbalance or mental illness can impact the greater community in ways that are detrimental to the survival and security of all, and the vision of humanity we wish to uphold. We are taking that into consideration on every level, and seek to protect you from the darkness you do not even know can exist."

It is such a different way of being in the world that I can barely even comprehend it. It is a model of community that speaks to the need to consider that one individual can indeed wreak havoc on a whole community's psychology in an instant. Laws and strict controls are created, Darlene explained to me, to attempt to avoid this and to protect the whole, even if it is at the cost of the individual.

Unfortunately, what this system seems to lack with its strong-arming is the other side of the spectrum. It also effectively restricts people from being able to have impact in positive ways. It disallows freedoms and motivations to be more generative in a culture that is in need of innovations. I don't bring any of this to the conversation with Darlene. I am more interested in hearing her perspective than sharing my own. I want to understand how the Cuban people think. I want to learn how they see their system through their own understanding. She has given me quite a lot to think about.

Perhaps one of the most fascinating contradictions to me here is the sense of hopelessness, and how that seems to give way to an ability to appreciate things that many of us take for granted. Albeit it can be a resigned acceptance; yet most Cubans have found an ability to be at peace in spite of their challenges. They have learned something that we in the USA would be wise to consider: the willingness to accept and enjoy life as it is, regardless of difficult conditions. Theirs is an ability to focus on the simple reality of what is, rather than wasting a lifetime complaining about it. Complaining will not change a thing, it just makes what you have to endure more painful for you and those around you. Cubans seem to really get that, possibly by forced coercion, but still, there is a certain wisdom in it.

I have been reading an incredible book, *Havana Reàl* by Yoani Sanchez, a Cuban woman, who started a blog called Generation Y. *(In Part 1 of this story, I have a segment entitled "Havana Reàl," that I titled years before I came upon her work, so when I happened across this book, it instantly called to me.)*

It is a fascinating read and has been giving me deep insight into Cuban life.

She writes, *"A widespread call to inaction, in the name of preserving mental hygiene, has taken over Cubans' ability to act. The person who complains or demands is seen as "some kind of weirdo."*

People here have learned to find gratitude even in the midst of challenges. That is one of the things that makes this island so special. I absolutely understand Yoani's point as well. This way of being can effectively incapacitate a culture to create change. It supports things staying the same, in a system that is desperately calling for change.

Nothing changes if nothing changes.

It demonstrates to me the two faces of Cuba. One being tired, with a worn down mentality that has been forced into surrendering, seeing no point in complaining about things that they do not believe they can ever change.

The other face is smiling and seeking joy in the ordinary. Choosing to preserve "mental hygiene" rather than ruining one's life by being eternally frustrated by the simple reality of life being as it is. This face shines with resilience, and truly reflects an enlightened attitude towards life.

Cuba's Next President?

"**I am going to** be the next president of Cuba," he tells me.

I cannot deny the statement gets my attention. He sits next to me, a cigarette hanging out of his lips, his face deeply lined with a maze of small wrinkles that cover strong Spanish features. He is a handsome man, suave and sophisticated with a casual air that keeps him approachable. We met dancing salsa at a bar on Calle Obispo with green vines dangling from the rafters in an open air patio.

"I am politico," he says as if I should do a backflip for him. He is eager to talk with me, and very interested in the fact that I am an American. He invites me to a table for a drink and a smoke. I am intrigued enough to take time off the dance floor to hear what he wants to share with me.

"The Cuban people need a new leader. I have many people who think like I do here who support me. Four months ago, I went to Washington, DC to talk to Barack Obama. I talked to two senators to tell them I am the right person for them to look to in Cuba. Fidel is eighty-two, his brother has not yet thought about a successor. The people are ready for a new leader. I am ready for them. I am ready to work with your country."

I was fascinated, if not convinced. To even speak of something like this in public in Cuba can be dangerous. I found myself looking over my shoulder a few times wondering if this was a setup for me somehow, and felt again like a character in a movie. He seemed quite comfortable and confident talking like this in public. He continued as if he sensed my apprehension.

"I do not fear death. I am not afraid to die for my people. I love my country. My people here need to be allowed to evolve." He takes a long drag on his cigar and gazes across the bar letting the thought linger between us.

After only one week here talking to people, I know this is true. I also know that everyone here loves their country, in spite of all the problems and issues. Many people I have talked to even said they love Fidel. They believe he is a good man and that he saved Cuba in many ways. There are many I have met who said they would fight to the death to save Fidel's Cuba and that the young generation will be lost when Fidel goes. I discovered a stark contrast to the stories we hear in the USA that every Cuban wants to leave Cuba. I found that equally as many want to stay. For as many that want change, I met just as many who did not.

"One day in the future, maybe in ten years, you will see my face on TV and remember me. I will be Cuba's salvation and take my people into a new prosperity. Cuba is strong, my people are intelligent. I have many supporters in your country who are helping me. Do you dance?" The question catches me off guard. I smile, and give him my hand.

"Claro, dale Presidente," I say to him. He smiles, stands and walks me three steps away from the table and navigates me beautifully through a cha cha cha.

We dance several more dances before the band stops. He walks me to the corner of my street, embraces me warmly, then backs away and shakes my hand. We turn and go our separate ways. I wonder if in a few years I will see a new face on some political propaganda in Cuba and remember this night. I realize I forgot to ask his name. I am almost glad that I did. I am sure I will never forget his face or those dark, piercing eyes.

Reflections of A Global Citizen

I am participating in the community of the entire world.
I wander.
I watch.
I listen.
I often feel like a ninja warrior priestess
in the city of the world
on a lifetime quest for understanding humanity.

A Global Citizen: The world is my domain

I have heard it said that what we teach and bring to the world is that which we need for ourselves first and foremost. I believe it to be true. My life's purpose being that of working to support, create and foster a sense of culture and community wherever I am, I can not help but recognize the reality of the relevance in my life. I am rich and blessed in many ways, with beautiful connections and friends around the world. Still, in moments, I feel like I am the most alone person on the planet.

My heart longs for something that feels always fleeting: a feeling of "belonging" with others that can really only come from our roots, family and cultural connections. I see the contrast with my own cultural identity everywhere here in Cuba. The people here know who they are and are not spending their lives seeking some illusionary "someday." They know where they come from. Most of them know they aren't going anywhere so they are forced to find contentment where they are.

They have a connection to their culture, to their community, and to their families. They have roots that go back through generations that they are still in touch with every day through their religion, their songs, and their dances. In contrast, most of my friends and family members do not even know where their grandparents came from, much less their ancestors before them. For many of us in the modern world, the cords were cut and little was revealed, preserved or shared through the generations. As so often happens, in the name of progress, the past is steamrolled and buried.

My cultural conditioning combined with my passion for travel and exploration lends me to being a bit of a loner in this world. I see myself as a self-proclaimed, fully discovered, lost, yet totally found, global citizen. Enlightened in many ways from my experiences traveling the world, I am fully connected to my spirit and soul. Even still, I am always aware of a deeper longing for a sacred something that my lifestyle, and cultural indoctrination, keeps always just outside of my grasp. Something that people here seem to have without question.

Being a single woman, with the passion for experience, knowledge and wisdom that I have, I am participating in the community of the entire world. I wander. I watch. I listen. I often feel like a ninja warrior priestess in the city of the world, on a lifetime quest for understanding humanity as a participant of many cultures. I am quite aware that I have the *privilege* of being able to live the life that I live. It does not escape me that being born in the USA as a woman, at the specific time that I was, plays a huge role in my ability to move between the worlds and choose this lifestyle. I am grateful that I was blessed enough to be born into a culture that does grant me, if nothing else, the freedom to create myself and my life as I please.

I am, indeed, a global citizen. I have home, friends, community and love everywhere.

Yet, in quiet moments, like now, sitting by the Malecón at sunset listening to the surf, watching the day come to a close, the tender soft place in me, as a woman, wants nothing more than the sanctuary of one good man to lean on. I lie myself down on the concrete wall, stretch out my legs, close my eyes and let myself dream.

Rhythm Bondage: Dance Addicts Grace

Tied too long to a tether too short
I am writhing in the ecstasy of demise
making love sweetly to the beast inside
Like a wild thing on the prowl
She moves me...She soothes me
She captures my spirit my soul
Makes me whole
I am tattered and battered by her incessant desire
She lifts me once again
I fly ever higher..
In the distance, the dancer moves closer
Awaiting this treasure
I am already claimed
It is unquestionably true
I am yours even though you can never be mine...
There is no one else for me but you
You are the unholdable, the unshakeable, the untakeable
The one always to be shared and adored
Pure rhythm and groove and eloquent by design
You tickle my body and deepen my mind
You enhance and romance me
Ignite me delight me

Incite me, in spite of me
You are my haven
My sanctuary of grace
Where hair twirling
Feet stomping
Booty shaking bliss
Make me miss you the moment that you walk away...
Baby just stay with me
All through the night
To twirl me eternally
through our heart's shared inner sight
I feel you in some way
I've not known before.
I'll wait for you always forevermore
I have no choice but to surrender
You are my life and my death
I am the addict
Your faithful loyal whore
Always here awaiting your bittersweet breath
My heart aches in the dawn's twilight's callings
Spinning circles into circles
Etching eternal memories thru my body's movement in time
Please don't stop the music
My heart whispers to the Gods of time
Please keep me here
In the arms of these angels
touching what I know within you is mine
Magic moves me
I can only surrender
This passion consumes me
Prisoner to its tender deepening hole
Happily strapped to the tether too tight
Knowing my bondage is somehow also my delight.

Bailar d'Amor: The Dance of Love

He shows up dressed head to toe in white.

His sharp features and jet black skin contrasted by the whites are stunning. He takes my hand and leads me to the dance floor.

I feel like a queen with her king, performing before the court.

I *am awake for* a long time feeling his warm, strong, perfect body next to mine. My eyes love to feast on the sculpted lines of his dark body in contrast to the white sheets draped across our bodies. His skin is soft, supple and stretched perfectly over strong developed muscles. He is a work of art. His body is a sculpture. He is a perfect model of maleness. My mind runs through the memories of last night. I can still feel the bliss in my body from dancing for hours together, twirling in rhythmical ecstasy together in perfect time. Dancing with him is so easy, so fun and so effortless. I disappear in the music with him and am carried and lifted into new levels in every turn. Our passion play in the dance is our world of escape from the mundane into the magical together. I have never before been met by a man in this way. He is strong, smart, sexy and looks after me in a way no other man has. My eyes trace the fullness of his parted lips as he sleeps next to me. I can not resist taking them in mine and stirring him into the day. He pulls me into him and we greet the morning together.

We both know what this relationship is, and what it isn't. The dance is the fuel that ignites our shared passion. We are here in Cuba together to dance and enjoy a few days as friends and lovers, nothing more. What connects us is much bigger than physicality, it is a deeper love for the music, the dance, and his culture. Neither of us is ready for something serious, and we have agreed to simply supporting each other through our healing processes after our respective break ups. Yet, seeing him here, in his home country, so comfortable and confident makes him even more attractive. It is a side of him I never got to see in the states. Our whole relationship there took place on the dance floor at social events, or in quiet moments together sharing bottles of wine on my porch under the moon, almost always talking about Cuba. I love seeing how he interacts with his family and culture here. It is truly beautiful.

When he gets up and starts to dress, my heart sinks a little. I want him to stay here with me all day. He is ready for his day, well rested, and off for a day to help his family in every way he can while he is here. I admire the fact that he is a man who prioritizes appropriately. He is not here just to enjoy time with me, after all. He is here for his family first. I am also here for my own journey. We planned to spend some time together on this trip, but it is not like we are only here to be with each other and we both know it. I am not at all interested in requiring more of his time or energy than he is willing to share. For Cubans there is nothing more important than family. This is a quality I respect and appreciate.

Hours later we met for an afternoon matinee show at Casa de Música in Havana. Located in Central Havana, this is a place for true salsa lovers, where dancing aficionados come in the evening to show their skills. Casa de Música hosts the island's most prestigious ensembles on a regular basis. It is spacious, with two floors, both with views of the stage, and three bars spread throughout the enclosure. Every city in Cuba has its own Casa de Musica. They are all governmen-run establishments that provide approved entertainment. Both local Cubans and tourists frequent Casa de Músicas throughout Cuba. Tourists have been flocking to the island since Cuba has been Cuba to enjoy music. The rich mix of Spanish and African musical traditions has gained Cuba a reputation as one of the premiere destinations in the world for top-tier dancing and quality music.

In Havana, Casa de Música offers matinee concerts that start at 5 pm, and later ones at 10 pm. We are at the matinee which is often considerably cheaper than the later show. Since Carlos will inevitably be paying for the whole family's entrance and drinks, it is a wise choice.

Carlos is accompanied by several members of his family, some of whom I have met at his family's home, and some I have not yet been introduced to. They all greet me with open arms, and smiles, drawing me in with love as part of their extended family. Carlos is dressed head to toe in white, as usual. I have never seen a more handsome, regal looking man. His sharp features and dark skin against the whites are stunning.

I dance several dances with his cousin, Yankel, before Carlos gives me a nod and extends his hand to me. We are the only two on the dance floor. I feel like a queen with her king performing before the court. All eyes are on us, and we both know it. Talking quiets as we claim the space together, elegantly moving together wrapped in our own cocoon of passion play. His family all stand quietly witnessing our moment, sharing with us energetically. He is a highly skilled dancer, always suave, strong, and clear in his guidance. His sister told me he trained hard as a child in Cuba, dancing in shows and performances, and studying the dance for all of his years before he went to the United States. It was his life, she told me. The smile on his face as we dance is medicine to my heart. We dance three dances. The whole time I have known him, I have never seen him look so happy, proud and fulfilled.

I notice that we dance together much better now than we ever have. Our bodies know each other much more intimately. Somehow just by being in Cuba together, we know and trust each other more on the dance floor and our dancing has evolved to a much higher level together. There is more freedom, more love, more of everything good between us. The chemistry is magical and the dancing is addictive.

When the dances end, I float back to my chair to ground myself. I am only granted a few short moments before someone else grabs my hand and twirls me back into bliss. The bottles of rum never stop coming. The night passes far too fast.

Hours later, after dropping his sister off at her house, he casually and quietly says to me, "What are you doing to me?"

All I could manage to say is, "I do not know but I think it is happening to me too." We are silent for the rest of the drive back to my room. He puts his hand on my thigh, and I place my hand on top of his. The energy in our hands feels like it is coming directly from our hearts.

He is already asleep when I get to bed after a shower to wash off the man sweat and cigar smoke from the bar. He has only stayed with me a few nights, and I am grateful for his company tonight. I curl myself around his perfect body and pray. I find myself staying awake all night just to feel him next to me and hear him breathe. I want time to stop, at least for a day or two just to be here in this perfect moment next to this man who dances me into bliss and loves me in a way I have never known. I want to stay suspended here in this peace and contentment for as long as I possibly can. I fight back tears and accept the reality that this love is nearing its completion. When he leaves Cuba, I have to let him go and let this part end. There really is no other possibility to be considered, at least not right now. I know we both know this and as a single tear rolls onto his skin, he stirs slightly, and pulls me deeper into him. He falls back asleep with his smooth bald head against my chest.

If I died now, I would die content. Dawn will come too soon as always. Only three days left before he has to return to the States and I continue on in Cuba to study music and dance. I remind myself to keep my head clear, and my heart safe.

The Red Flag Parade

The red flag parade has begun.
My senses are alive. My mind is perplexed.

I retreat and find safe harbor in the dance.
I am home and always safe in the arms of my one true beloved:
The sanctuary of rhythm and movement.

The night invites me out for a walk to soothe my troubled mind. I run into my new friend, Mario, whom I met my first day in Havana. Mario works selling tourist trinkets at a little storefront near my casa. I liked him instantly for his openhearted candor. He engaged me effortlessly in such a natural, non pushy way and showed me some of the dance spots close to where I was living the first night we met.

He is easy going, suave, and not the kind of guy who is ever going to be annoying or pushy. He is a Cuban Rasta. His short spiky dreads popping up all over his head animate him as much as his joyful personality. He speaks perfect English, which is refreshing for me right now. My Spanish is getting better, but I still struggle a lot. Tonight my head and heart are both hurting, and I don't feel like struggling with the language barrier. Mario makes for a perfect companion for me, a safe space to disengage with my reality for a few hours.

Tonight, all I really want is to find a place to dance. Mario walks me through the streets of Havana Vieja. We share small talk, stories and lots of laughs, kicking plastic bottles like a soccer ball passed between us as we go. He takes me to a little corner bar with a railing around the outside a few blocks off of Calle Obispo. It's dark, dingy and fits my mood perfectly, except for the fact that it's totally empty and all I want is to drown myself in music and sweating, dancing bodies right now. I find myself hesitating to enter. Mario grabs my arm and pulls me inside with a huge smile as if we are at the best party in town. "Come on," he says.

"Salsa aquí Mario? There's no one here." I say to him a little disappointed that this is where we ended up. I'm in Havana. I want a full club, tightly packed with sweaty bodies, with music blasting my senses back into stillness. I want tons of sexy, steamy Cubans around me dancing and singing together with infinite options of great dancers and endless bottles of rum. This was not at all what I was envisioning for a night out dancing in Havana.

"No importa, bailas conmigo. Tranquila. You are sad tonight, I want to make you happy again." Mario says sincerely. "Maybe tonight, you will forget him and let me show you something else of Cuban men, my sister. What do you want to drink?" He is so proud to be here with me and share this with me.

I had really hoped I was hiding my grief, but Cubans seem to see everything no matter how good I think my facade is. I laugh out loud, a little nervous suddenly that I've been exposed. My new friend clearly sees right through me. I wonder if he can sense my disappointment at the venue being so empty too. I decide to stop being a jerk and just let the night unfold how it's meant to.

"Ok, ok Mario. Siete años, no hielo. I'll get us a table." I respond. I see the band enter with their instruments in the same moment and commit myself to enjoying the night for whatever it presents to me. I commit to letting go of my attachments to how I think Cuba should unfold for me.

His smile is all I need to know that I gave him a gift in that decision. "Con yooooo," he says to me with smiling eyes as he returns to the table with a glass of rum in one hand and a beer in the other.

"La pinga tuyo," I respond and he slaps his leg and his laughter lifts my spirits.

"Forget him tonight. It will pass. Cuban men are crazy sometimes. Don't worry, you will see it will pass." Mario says to me. "For tonight just dance, enjoy. Life is short, be happy."

He raises his beer bottle and I lift my glass of rum and we make a toast to the dance. This is why I am in Cuba after all, to dance and enjoy. I did not come here to deal with drama.

The band starts and as soon as the music hits me, I am at peace. My body takes over and the medicine of music takes the pain of my trampled heart away. I am happy and free. Time stops, my mind can be distracted and my natural state of joy returns.

Mario is a great dancer: skillful and strong. We are the only two dancing for the first few songs, but slowly over the set, Cubans come in, and start to dance. Lesson learned, trust my Cuban friends. I asked him to keep me away from the tourist spots, and he did just that. This is a local place where the Cubans come to drink and dance. I am the only tourist here and no one seems to even notice me. I'm grateful for that tonight.

Throughout the evening Mario seems to know exactly how to be there for me somehow. We dance, we laugh and we drink, then dance more. I am so glad that Mario is such a safe, and cheerfully comical character. He keeps bringing me back to laughter and lightheartedness any time my mind starts to slip into sadness. I am even more happy that he is such a great dancer.

Carlos is leaving in two days. My grief stuns and surprises me in light of the fact that he has disappeared into the maze of Cuba, and seemingly abandoned me after turning into some kind of strange insecure angry monster with me a few nights ago.

I am angry, hurt and deeply disgusted by the Dr. Jekyl-Mr. Hyde transformation I witnessed the other night in Carlos. The dignified beautiful man I was falling in love with fell into some kind of strange jealous rum-induced idiocy I have never seen the likes of before. It all feels like a bad dream. How did my heaven turn so quickly to hell? How did sweet so quickly turn to sour, bitter poison?

Tonight, I need the dance. Mario is safe for me because I am not even the least bit attracted to him, and I know he is not the kind of guy that would take advantage of me. He is a friend for me, a brother, a comfort, and an ally. There is zero sexual attraction between us and we both know already that romance is never going to be part of our friendship.

Tonight, I simply need the safe space and comfort that he so willingly provides me. I take it gratefully. He is totally respectful and kind. I know I have found a lifelong friend in this cheerful, dread headed, rasta, salsa dancing Cubano.

After dancing for hours and drinking way too much rum, we take a walk to the Malecón. I have no idea what time it is and I'm not at all interested in knowing. It's now and now is perfect. Like so many Cubans, Mario is super easy to be with. He is familial, silly, light hearted and always playful: the perfect medicine for my heavy heart. We walk the Malecón laughing and slapping each other on the back as we share dumb jokes, all the while making fun of anything and everything we can.

My Cuban cell phone rings. I let it ring for a while before I reluctantly answer. Carlos's voice is clearly agitated. Surprisingly, I find a sense of satisfaction in it.

"Where are you? What are you doing? Who are you with?" he barks through the phone at me.

I laugh as I answer him, "Whoa whoa whoa baby, slow down. How are you?" I have had just enough rum to not be able to take this seriously at the moment. I've been having so much fun with Mario, I'm not about to let him steal my joy. As always, I am just not interested in fighting at all.

"I'm taking a walk on the Malecón with my friend. What's up? Are you ok?" I respond to him flatly. Instantly, another stream of questions comes barking through the phone at me.

"Who is he? Are you replacing me already? You should go back to your house right now." He is angry and accusatory. I am calm and emotionally non-reactive, but inside I am furious and a little embarrassed wondering if Mario can hear this coming through the phone at me. I walk a distance away, giving Mario a little wave that I'll return when I'm done.

I skirt his questions intentionally. He screwed up. I am free in Havana, he's leaving in two days, and I'm not. I am enjoying a beautiful night under the moon with a friend, and there is nothing he can do about it.

"I am not going to fight with you. We can talk when you have calmed down. I will not deal with this Carlos. Goodnight." I hang up the phone. I feel a wave of mixed-up confusing emotions roll through me. I am strangely pleased that he finally called. Mostly, I am completely repulsed by his jealousy and befuddled by his quick flip of personalities. He went from being kind and nurturing, to possessive and jealous literally overnight. He is one day my lover, and the next day my enemy with no explanation or justification at all. Then he disappears completely for three days with no communication. Now he has the nerve to call me barking at me as if I am his disobedient child? I am frightened and turned off; and while I am frustrated by his disappearance in these past few days, I am actually grateful that he hasn't come back around. I don't really want to see him again. I wonder how I could have missed any red flags that would have warned me that he could become insane like this. I've scanned my memory for them over and over again and just can't see even one warning that he would be capable of this kind of behavior. What could I have missed?

I have no obligation to cater to his insane jealousy or insecurity. He is not my partner, boyfriend or husband, and even if he was, he has no right whatsoever to act in the way that he did towards me. We both know it.

When I saw him last, he was raging in jealousy and insecurity with no basis, no grounds and no explanation or conversation. We had planned a night out with his cousin and some friends at Casa de Música to see Los Van Van, a popular Timba group in Havana. He had left me at Casa de Música with his cousin, Yankel, telling us he had to go drop something off and he would be back in a few minutes. Yankel had become like a little brother to me the first night, and while I was happy to spend some time with him, the entire night he and I were waiting anxiously for Carlos to show back up so we could all enjoy the night together. Both Yankel and I were there to spend time with Carlos after all, not with each other.

The show was amazing of course. It was electric, and with a full house of dancing happy Cubans, Yankel and I, of course, had a great evening. Yet, the entire time there was this energy of waiting for Carlos, and that made it a little bit awkward for both of us. When Carlos finally showed up again, it was 2 am, the show was over, and he came back apparently only to drive us home. He then had the audacity to spend the whole drive from Vedado to Havana Vieja berating me, in front of Yankel, who sat silently in the back seat as Carlos wildly accused me of being with another man. He was cold, callous and completely out of line. There was no reasoning with him, and no talking him down. I was not even granted a moment to find out what was going on in his head. He was literally a different man than the one I had known up until that very moment. It was like someone or something else had control of him. My heart had completely retreated from him and in that moment, I knew there was no going back.

I have been refusing his countless calls since then, until now. Apparently, the red flag parade has begun. I am a wise enough woman to heed the warnings and pay close attention to them. While I am confused by his behavior, I also have no tolerance for it. In all the time I have known him, he has never been like this. In my experience, if someone is like this once, it only gets worse in time. I don't need it or want it in my life. I have heard enough stories about the Cuban and Latino jealousy to have learned plenty from other people's mistakes in my life. I didn't come to Cuba for this.

It is well known that Cubans can be excessively possessive, obsessive and jealous in romantic relationships. The old world values still exist and *machismo* in Cuba is still very alive and well. Women are still often treated like property and expected to behave, dress, respond and obey in the way that their men require. Cuban men are often overbearingly controlling and insecure, and often that is because they themselves are fooling around on the side. Equally as often, it is just deep insecurities. I have heard that the women can be the same, and that these ways are just "part of the culture". Jealousy, control, and high drama in relationships is "normal" in the culture, but since this is my first romance of any kind with a Cuban, I am inexperienced in knowing how to deal with it.

I am simply not interested in the drama he seems to be wanting to engage in. Getting out and going dancing was the best possible way for me to re-empower myself and feel good again. Dancing gives me a free space to process without thought. The music has its way of releasing trauma and reconnecting me with a grounded sense of self-worth and self-respect. It has been my sanctuary for many years, even before I discovered salsa dancing.

Moments in between dances are moments merely of existence. I can not deny that they often are almost a struggle. My life has been ruled by rhythm's bliss for so long now; I am sure I would wither and die without it. I would prefer to die than live without it, that much I know.

Nothing can ever take the place of the bliss of dancing. My body, my soul, my heart and my mind all crave the surrender. The anticipation of it can be consuming. I live for the suspension of the mundane into the magical playground of the groove. It is its own drug and it activates the pleasure centers of the brain much like any other intoxicant. The pleasure I get from it makes it worth anything I have to sacrifice to get my fix.

The voice of my culture and upbringing wants to shame me for playing in my secret world of dance. I am a single woman, staying out late at night, twirling ecstatically in the arms of seemingly infinite men. I am easily intoxicated in the dance, spiraling in, out and around, being pulled close then spun out, seeing and feeling the lover in each one of them throughout the night, for four to six minutes of wildly sensual passion through the dance. Yet, the energy and vitality, the almost ninja like focus it takes to let my body be moved across the floor by the will of another and to respond to his touch and guidance spontaneously are indeed addictive and a welcome relief from the daily grind.

So, what can I do? The only cure I can find is to seek another fix. I don't even want to be cured. Am I any better than a drug addict or an alcoholic? Not really. Some may call it a healthy addiction, but is it? I am driven night after night to seek out any place I can find to move in unison with others who share my affliction, spending money, time and incapable of leading a "normal" life anymore. I willingly surrender and accept my fate, addicted to this bliss. Intoxicated by the groove, the infection continues to spread through my body, mind and soul and I go willingly into the deep well of its source and offer myself to its infinite unfolding.

I return to Mario who is waiting patiently for me on the seawall. I know he probably heard Carlos yelling through the phone. He looks at me knowingly. I let him put his arm around me and hold me in my grief. I sink into him and feel comforted. My heart wants Carlos's arms around me, but my head knows it is over. The old classic rock song, "When you can't be with the one you love, love the one you're with," runs through my head and I sing it out loud. Mario and I laugh through my tears together. I feel grateful to have a brother next to me, a safe space in the midst of a whacky storm.

In that moment, I consciously chose to embrace the Cuban way more and more in my life. I chose to accept what is present for me in the moment rather than wasting any more tears on a man who cannot give me what I want or need; a man who is beginning to show signs of abusive tendencies that I simply cannot and will not tolerate. Mario is safe. He offers me, as a brother and friend, a healthy space in which to lick my wounds and begin to move on. I return my energy to our laughter and we continue our walk, laughing heartily about the stupidity of jealousy. Over the night I have shared almost everything about my relationship with Carlos with Mario, so he knows the whole story from the first dance up until the last.

We indulge ourselves in companionship and friendship walking through the living museum of Havana all night long. Havana is so magical at night. The majesty of the buildings emerges even more in the darkness when you cannot see the flaking paint and broken windows. The past comes alive in the heart of night. You can almost feel the ghosts whirling around, haunting the city with the zillions of dreams and desires that this place is filled with.

I find myself being able to be happy in spite of my grief, hurt and confusion. Mario walks me home. At my stairwell, he slaps me on the back lightly, says "Cojone, get some sleep, it's almost morning." We laugh and I watch him walk down the marble staircase, intrigued by the light drifting up through the door making magic out of a dark dingy staircase. I am able to sleep for a few hours knowing that letting go of Carlos is the best possible thing for me to do in every way.

Finding Food

The morning air is refreshing. My heart is aching and if I wasn't here in Cuba, I might just lay around in bed crying over spilt milk. Fortunately, I am well distracted knowing I have a fun companion to spend the day with. I am on a mission to find food today so I do not have to rely on eating at overpriced restaurants all week. Mario agreed to help me and show me where I can get what I need.

He meets me exactly on time at the cafe at the corner of Plaza Vieja. I buy two coffees for us to enjoy before going on our adventure.

"I hear all the time Mario, that there is no food in Havana, and that people are starving here. Is that true?" I asked him.

"Havana has everything. You just have to know where to look, and you have to have money to buy it. You can eat caviar and drink the most expensive champagnes if you know the right people and have enough money to pay for it." He laughs. He has this way of making light of the most serious situations. I know it is his way of dealing with the somber reality of his world. His dreads shake on his head as he lights up a cigarette and looks across the Plaza.

"Here in Cuba, it is propaganda they speak. No one here is starving. Not really. Some people are not getting very good nutrition because what the state gives us is not always enough. We rarely get rations for fresh things like fruits and vegetables. Most people do not make enough money to buy extra things, so we have to find ways you know. But starving?" He laughs again, his eyes twinkling in frustrated compassion for his people,

"Not one of us here will let another one starve. If he doesn't have food, someone will feed him. That is how we are." His energy sobers a bit and as he draws on his cigarette his eyes glaze over a little bit.

I could sense the sadness in his voice as he went on. "During the Special Period[4], things were very bad. I was very young, but I remember always being hungry then. I do not like to think about it." His joyful nature returned quickly as he changed the subject.

"Mira, dale mami. I want to show you how we Cubans get our food, and after, you can buy the things you need at the market. It is something of Cuban culture that you should know about." From his pocket, he pulls out a small black book tied with a shoestring. He explains to me that this is his ration book. He opens it up and shows it to me.

"In this book, every week, they mark when I go to pick up food. There is a line for meat, cheese, rice, you see? Vamos, I'll show you. I am going today to get food. Dale, dale, dale. Vamos." He claps his hands cheerfully and leads the way. I put my arm through his and skip along like a little girl with her big brother taking her on a great adventure into a new world.

We walk out of the tourist area of Havana Vieja into what I affectionately refer to as *"Havana Reàl." Havana Reàl* is the vast maze of slums that showcase barely standing buildings, staircases reinforced by rotting wood and metal scraps, and piles of dog poop that inspire you to keep your eyes down, watching your every step.

We approach a small line of people waiting patiently for their meat rations. They are all holding dirty plastic bags that look well used. These bags will transport the meat home for them, be washed

---

4   *The Special Period* was a very difficult time for Cubans during the late '90s. It was an extended period of economic crisis that began in 1991 primarily due to the dissolution of the Soviet Union and, by extension. The economic depression of the Special Period was at its most severe in the early to mid-1990s, before slightly declining in severity towards the end of the decade, once Hugo Chávez's Venezuela emerged as Cuba's primary trading partner and diplomatic ally, and especially after the year 2000 once Cuba-Russia relations improved under the presidency of Vladimir Putin.

It was defined primarily by extreme reductions of rationed foods at state-subsidized prices, the severe shortages of hydrocarbon energy resources in the form of gasoline, diesel, and other petroleum derivatives that occurred upon the implosion of economic agreements between the petroleum-rich Soviet Union and Cuba, and the shrinking of an economy overdependent of Soviet imports.

and reused until they fall apart. There are bars on the windows of the storefront and a big door is swung open wide to reveal a man standing behind a flat concrete counter smoking a cigar and drinking a tiny jar of black coffee. Mario hands him his ration book. The man checks off the date, and scribbles in it before handing it back to my friend.

I am touched by the friendliness and spirit of everyone in line. Everyone is laughing and making jokes. Mario is gregarious and brings his playful spirit to the scene. I watch as the man behind the counter cuts off a few chunks of meat from a big round wheel of meat for my friend and puts it in his bag. This is his ham for the week. It looks more like a large fat strange hotdog than actual ham. It is some kind of processed food product rather than true meat, I am quite sure of that. I would be afraid to eat it after it has been sitting out for who knows how long, unrefrigerated and touched by who knows how many hands, and dirty, unsanitized knives. My western conditioning would have me starving here in no time if I were a meat eater. Thankfully, being a vegetarian, I am able to bypass that stress.

Mario takes his rations with a big smile, pats the others in line on the back cordially, and we re-enter the street. We continue our journey through Havana Reàl on to another market he wants to show me where fruits and vegetables can be purchased.

"This market I am taking you to now, Cheri, do not ever come down here at night. This is a dangerous place at night, people come here for cocaine."

I wonder if I heard him right, but right away, he makes a big sniff holding one nostril.

"You know cocaine right? It makes the people crazy." He changes his gait and stumbles around making his eyes big, bulgy and crazy looking.

We both laugh hysterically. Unconsciously, I notice that I reach for my bag, suddenly feeling vulnerable alone with Mario in his world, so far away from anyone I know in mine. For a fleeting moment my all too familiar fear programming hits me. I wonder suddenly if I am being taken into a trap. Has he been setting me up to be robbed this whole time? What if all the propaganda about Cuba being dangerous is true, and I am just being conned?

I choose to not accept that thought as a possibility, and relax my grip on my bag. I know that this man is genuinely a good person. I let out a facetious "Oh my god! Where are you taking me? I am so scared!"

He stops and looks at me in amazement. My sarcasm clearly surprises him. He laughs and puts his arm around me. We walk together as kindred souls in his world. The market is bustling and offers all the food I am looking for at Cuban peso prices. I buy a large *fruta bomba*5, a pineapple, tomatoes, bananas, greens and all my produce for the week. I spend the equivalent of $4. For me this is an incredible deal. Back home, just the pineapple would have cost me that much or more. For my friend, who makes the equivalent of $12 a month teaching school full time, buying fresh fruits and veggies is a luxury rarely to be afforded. I offered to buy him whatever he wanted, and tried to give him some of what I bought, but he politely refused me.

---

5   In Cuba, *fruta bomba* is the fruit also known as papaya. It is wise to use caution with the word papaya in Cuba as it also has a connotation of meaning a woman's vagina.

Rhumba

The drums echo against the walls creating a cascading cacophony of sound and vibration in the small, tightly packed patio. Sweat pours off of my forehead, my clothes are soaked and stuck to me. I can barely move, yet I am dancing even still. It is impossible to stand still when the rhythm is this good and this strong. Mario stands next to me laughing and joking with me nonstop as he leans against the bar behind him. A bodacious, gorgeous black woman dressed in skintight red pants and a white cotton crop top floats over in perfect rhythm, and engages him in the dance. I watch the two of them connect and enter the world of rhumba together, both masterful in the dance, alive and sensually playing and flirting through their movements to the drums.

Everywhere around the room, voices lift together with the chorus of the songs, their voices responding to the singer of the percussion ensemble in effortless harmony. The drums are fierce, and fast, yet sensual and hypnotic. The *clave*[6] drives the rhythm as it pierces through the drums in the hands of a skilled player who also is singing the lead. A line of six drummers pound out song after song, moving from slow to fast then back to slow. They are working the crowd into rhythmical bliss with each song. Here, we are all part of the magic. We are making this rhumba happen together. The energy is powerful

---

6   The instrument *clave* consists of two short round hard wood sticks that are played against each other in a repetitive pattern that defines the time signature, pulse, and genre of the music. In Cuban music, the *clave* is the time keeper or the "key" to the song. There are many different patterns and each genre of music has it's own defining *clave*: Son, Rhumba, Bembe, etc.

and captivating. I am beyond joyous to be here in the midst of this in the middle of the day with Mario and his friends.

Mario has been helping me to find inroads into the non touristy more rootsy, authentic music of Havana. He's told me that reggaeton is taking over and the rhumbas and salsa events are becoming harder to find than they were a few years ago. A space in front of the drummers has been cleared and couples take turns showing off their moves in front of the crowd. The rest of us watch, clap and enjoy. It is a true community sharing, there is no judgment or politics here. This is just Cubans being together, sharing in their cultural heritage, and having a great Sunday afternoon sweating, dancing, singing and entering the trance of rhythm church together. I feel so honored to be here. I love that no one seems to care or notice that I'm a foreigner.

The word Rhumba (also sometimes spelled Rumba) is actually more or less a generic term that comes from the verb *rumbear* which means going to parties, dancing, and having a good time. So in essence, a Rhumba is a party of sorts. In Cuba it is usually a party where skilled drummers drive participants into high energy parties where participants and musicians join together singing, dancing and enjoying their cultural roots. Rhumbas and Guaguancó quite often go hand in hand as they are today on this patio.

Guaguancó is an Afro-Cuban music and dance form that has a very distinct melody in the drum parts with a clave, shekere, and playful spontaneous lyrics that tell stories and invoke flirtations.

It originated during the slave era in the 1800s as a way for the Africans to both celebrate their culture, and have some fun. Traditionally, the women wore the big Spanish style skirts, which made the visual presentation very sensual and seductive. The woman's role was to flirt, and engage, but to always protect that which was under her skirt from the male's pursuit.

Guaguancó is in essence a courtship dance of sorts, and almost always becomes somewhat of a sexually charged competition between the male and female. The male periodically attempts to *catch* his partner with a single thrust of his pelvis. This pelvic throughst, called the vacunao is meant to symbolize sexual penetration. The vacunao can also be expressed by the hand or foot. The woman's job is to always stay one step ahead to keep him from the *catch*. The dance and the energy around it is always fun, lighthearted and playful in nature.

In modern times, women rarely wear the big white skirts unless it is for a performance, but most Cubans know how to dance Guaguancó and it is one of the favorite dances of the island. Now, women will use a scarf or nothing but their bare hand to block the male's efforts to catch her off guard in the dance.

Little is more fun in Cuba than a good old fashioned rhumba. Mario and I stay until the very end watching couple after couple step into the center of the room to showcase their skills. When we leave, it feels as if we have been reborn. The world seems brighter. I feel lighter, more alive and completely connected from the inside out.

A Dangerous Cuban Cocktail: Rum y Cubano Loco

When I get back to my room, I see that Carlos has called three times. I am glad I left my phone in the room to give myself some space from him today. I know what he will say will just disappoint me again. I really do not want to hear it. The phone rings from a number I do not recognize. Stupidly, I answer. The same questions come flying at me again.

"Where are you? What are you doing? Go home. Have you been drinking? Someone told me you were with someone last night." The agitation and jealousy is wild in him. It is eating him up that I have not been answering and that I am not bowing to his commands.

I am intolerant, and uncharacteristically short with him. "I do not know what is going on with you love, but I do not have energy for this." I hang up on him. His drama is absurd and far-fetched: as if anyone he knows here would somehow know me in Havana and just happen to see me in this huge city. It is ludicrous. I am again repulsed by the immaturity of his drama.

I know he is bluffing. I do not like it, not at all. I find it trivial, annoying, and unnecessary drama. The saboteur is clearly running rampant in him. I make a mental note to be very careful with this situation.

A few hours later, my phone rings again. I do not answer, and it rings again and again and again. Finally, after fifteen rings, I pick it up and say nothing.

He speaks a little more calmly this time.

"Where are you? Who are you with? I am coming to Havana. Do you want to see me before I go?" He asks me. The way he speaks is more like a command than a question though, and it catches me off guard. Who has this man become here? He has become increasingly demanding, obsessive, jealous, controlling and downright difficult to get along with in these past few days. I feel like I am dealing with an emerging psychotic personality suddenly. I do not answer his commanding questions. Instead, I remain silent, trying to make sense of it all. I am beginning to understand some of the things people have said to me in the past few years about the crazy Cuban men. As much as I adore Carlos, I don't want anything to do with drama.

"Meet me at 6:30 at Casa de Música. I will see you there. I want to talk to you." The line goes silent.

I am baffled and repulsed by his behavior and the manner in which he spoke to me. Yet some place in me feels sadness and compassion for his self-created suffering. The wise woman in me says, *"Do not even bother going, it is going to be a disaster."* I can feel the tension between us like a tightly strung wire ready to snap. I feel particularly volatile in my disgust at his behavior. A bolt of adrenaline that screams *fight or flight* surges through me. Yet, I know I will go, out of respect, to say goodbye to him if nothing else. The fighter in me and the lover in me are both called to the court equally.

At 6:30 exactly, he shows up dressed from head to toe in red. I sense the energy of Chango ready for a battle tonight. Chango is the Orisha (god) of thunder and lightning in the Yoruba Religion that birthed Santería in Cuba. He is a warrior, fierce and jealous, yet also very loyal and devoted to those he loves. One of the most respected, and feared, of the Orishas, Chango's color is red and he carries the power of the cosmos in his fury and his passion. He is quick to anger, and can be impulsive and over reactive.

Carlos almost always dresses in all white. I am slightly disturbed that he is wearing all red tonight. It seems like he is ready for a fight, like he is summoning Chango within him. He embraces me with a strange smirk on his face then backs away from me. He is slurring as if his tongue has been stung by anesthesia. I wonder if he went to the dentist and got a shot or a tooth pulled.

"Did you go to the dentist today?" I said to him, genuinely curious. "Why are you slurring like that?"

"I drunk," he says. I laugh, not yet having any idea of the drama that is in store for me tonight because of his drunkenness.

Like a blade cutting through the air between us, I sense a coldness inside him that feels savage, maybe even dangerous. Everything in my body suddenly alerts to a part of him I had not known existed. I am simultaneously compassionate, scared and strangely intrigued by a burning curiosity on what could possibly have made him so upset.

Inside the bar, he buys a bottle of rum, and a bottle of water for me. He is drunk and clearly plans on getting more drunk. The rum, the music, the dancing and the drama combine into a dangerous Cuban cocktail the likes of which I never could have imagined. He lets me into what's been going on as the drama of the night begins. What comes out of his mouth blows my mind, breaks my heart and shocks me all at once.

"You kissed my cousin. We can be friends, but we are through. I see how you are now. Now I know about you." He is pointing at me, making false accusations out of thin air, and acting crazy.

My first instinct is to laugh, but I realize he actually believes this nonsense. He is genuinely hurt since he actually believes his own crazy story. Finally, for the first time since the night he left me with Yankel at Casa de Música, I am getting a glimpse of what has been going on in his mind for the past few days. He thinks I made out with Yankel, his younger cousin. This, of course, never happened. There has never been even a passing thought of being with another man. Not even for a minute.

I do my best to try to keep it light, and I cannot help but to laugh out loud. The accusation is so wrong and so out of left field for me, it's just silly to me.

"Whoa, whoa, whoa amor. What are you talking about? I did not kiss anyone. I for sure would not make out with your cousin. He's like a little brother to me. What are you thinking? Please stop this and let's just enjoy our last night together. You're really wrong about this, Carlos. Let it go."

The rest of the night becomes a torturous slow dance with his demons: I move towards him with love and compassion, trying to find a way to reach him, and he backs away from me as if I have leprosy. All night long, he looks at me with daggers of fire shooting through me from his eyes over countless glasses of rum. I am innocent and unaffected, but something in my heart breaks for his suffering.

I find myself feeling a deep compassion for this insecurity that he suffers with. I have been there before. I know what a horrible experience it is to feel jealous. I know how terrible it feels to feel like the person you trusted with your heart and body has betrayed you, but in my case, sadly, it was true. Carlos is suffering over something that has no basis in reality whatsoever. It does not matter that what he thinks is absolutely not true. In his world, he feels it as true right now. There is nothing I can do but let him move through it. Nothing I say will matter right now. Yet, in spite of my compassionate heart, I am disgusted by this drama. Knowing he is leaving tomorrow, this is the last thing I want to be dealing with tonight. All I want right now is to leave. My keys and bag are locked in his car. When I ask him for the keys to get my things and go home, he refuses, leaving me stuck.

Finally he takes my hand and we dance. It is one of the most incredible dances of my life. I feel like we could dance life into creation or destroy the world in a moment. I am not sure if we are fighting or surrendering to love in the dance. We dance with a fury I have never felt, matched with a profound passionate love and tenderness that seems unending. We dance together perfectly, matching every step, unified in the thing that connects us beyond the drama, the respect and love of the dance. For a few moments I think maybe this night can transform. Maybe the dance will work its magic to release his insanity. The very moment that thought enters my mind, as if on cue, he passes me off to his cousin. My heart sinks again. Even the dance cannot reach him here.

Eventually, he agrees to get me home, which is all I've been wanting to do since this night began. I get into the car in the back seat. Yankel quietly gets into the driver's seat. I am grateful for a sober driver. I feel sorry for Yankel. I know that Carlos has been treating him poorly also in his delusional beliefs. He is family, however, and I am guessing he's seen this all before.

For most of the ride back to my room, Carlos continues accusing me of kissing Yankel, rambling on incoherently in the car and cursing me at the same time. In all my life, I have never dealt with such senseless drama.

"Tranquillo Carlos, no pasa nada. Estas equivocado primo mío." (Relax Carlos, Nothing happened. You are wrong, my cousin.) Yankel is quiet but it's obvious he's pretty frustrated too. Carlos can not hear anything but his own sick thoughts taking him farther into his own self-created hell.

I feel once again like a character in a movie. A really bad B-rated movie. This is all so surreal and such a sick twist to this trip. It is so contradictory to my life, who I am, and what I am all about. All of it is just purely surreal. Is this really happening? Who's running the camera? Where is the film crew? This is an absolutely perfect movie scene for some stupid drama in someone else's life. Surely it cannot be mine, and yet, it is.

On a deeper level, I can feel compassion for his suffering. Obviously, he has feelings he is afraid of. He has sabotaged our last night and let his demons of fear and jealousy win because he lacks the emotional maturity to do anything else. I am dumbfounded and traumatized over the way the night unfolded. I am sad that I can never trust him fully again in the same way. Tonight is the final red flag I can not ignore. I am glad he is leaving in the morning.

His cousin drops us off at my casa for the night, and takes the car. He will return in a few hours to take Carlos to the airport. Carlos stumbles up the stairs to my room, with apologies starting to pour from his mouth with each slow step up the three flights of stairs to my room. I am in shock at the quick reversal as the beast in him finally tires of its fight and the truth begins to emerge.

"I'm sorry baby. I know you didn't do anything wrong. I believe you. I'm sorry. I love you baby. I'm so scared you are going to find someone else here in Cuba when I leave. I want to hold you. I missed you so much. I'm scared baby. I'm sorry. I am going to miss you so much."

I put him into my bed and went to the shower. I stay in the hot water for a long time washing this whole nasty night off of me. When I get back to the bed he is snoring. I push him over and lie down with my back to him. I feel cold even next to his warm body.

A few hours later, he wakes, vomits in a plastic bag and dresses to leave.

I walk him to the door, feeling complete with my own knowing that this relationship is over. I am repulsed by his actions and words, and I am sad that this is how it has to end. He asks me to accompany him to the street to wait for his ride. I decide he does not deserve my companionship. He deserves to stand there alone, waiting for his ride, hungover, feeling like death at dawn after vomiting into a plastic bag, thinking about what he has destroyed.

"Thanks for helping me out with things here. Goodbye." I say to him.

"I'll see you back in the States," he says, "I had a good time with you here in Cuba," he says meekly trying to fix the unfixable.

"Don't count on it, Carlos. Have a safe trip home. Goodbye."

I turn my face when he attempts to kiss me goodbye, then turn my back to him and walk back up the stairs to my room. I am more than clear that I will not go back for another round. I need to learn the lesson of letting go, walking away and not looking back. Cuba is the perfect place to practice non-attachment.

I know enough to know it would have only gone downhill from here. I do not need to waste another minute of my time on a man who shows such clear signs of becoming unstable, abusive or hurtful. I run through the night in my head several times trying to make sense of it all only to come to the conclusion that there is no sense to be made of it. It's impossible to make sense out of crazy. I think about the number of things he did last night alone that hurt me. I remind myself that I deserve more respect. It is only the tip of an iceberg I do not want to see rolling around causing chaos in my life.

It does not matter why he acted like that, or what created his behavior. It's not my job to fix him. What matters is for me to be smart enough to walk away and to take it for what it was. I commit myself to leaving this drama in Cuba and staying away from him when I get home. I am grateful that it will be three months or more before I return.

I find one of my earrings in the bed and when I try to fix it, it breaks completely. I throw it in the trash. The metaphor is not lost on me: I need to do the same thing with this man.

He is broken. I can not fix him. There is no potential for a healthy relationship with him. I need to toss it aside and walk away without another thought.

I have the whole of Cuba before me to explore after all, and everywhere I look there are beautiful men who can dance me into euphoria.

Where one door closes, another will open and a brighter light will shine.

Part 2: Trinidad

Plays of light dance across a village brilliantly speckled with red terra cotta roofs and soft pastels that shamelessly reveal its colonial history.

Framed by azure seas and rolling green mountains a small pueblo sprawls into the hills.

Within is a world where the music never stops, and history still sings with passion through the eternal haunting choirs and hypnotic rhythms of a rich African heritage.

Named as a World UNESCO city in 1988, Trinidad's well-preserved narrow streets, plazas and cathedrals give us a looking glass back to the height of the 19th century sugar boom.

Wander through cobblestone streets alive with antiquity, where the soft clicking of horse hooves is a constant backdrop to life's unfoldings.

Take in the artistry and indulge yourself in the lost art of handmade crafts and Trinidad's famous fabrics.

Discover the rich Campesino culture. Venture to the mountains for a taste of mountain grown, fresh roasted coffee served with the gracious heart of Cuban generosity.

Delight in cascading waterfalls that plunge into refreshing pools of fresh mountain water.

Find yourself floating in the crystal blue seas of Playa Ancon as the simple life begins to breathe its beauty into you.

Welcome to Trinidad [7]

---

7   This segment was written by Cheri Shanti for a TV documentary series entitled *The Beauty of Cuba* in 2017

Finding Home
In Trinidad

Bliss has found me again. I have entered a new world where colonial architecture, cobblestone streets, horses, farmers, fishermen, musicians, dancers and artists of all kinds create a unique tapestry of life. A picturesque town framed by azure seas and rolling green mountains in the heart of nature. I am sensually embraced from head to toe, from the inside out. Oya sings to me through the ethers. The moon shines down from a ghostly clouded sky as the music moves me. I've found what I've always felt that I had been missing. I feel at home more than I ever have anywhere. I have only been here a few hours, but I know this place will hold my heart forevermore. In this little pueblo, 4 hours from Havana, I have discovered a world filled with all of my favorite things in the world in one place: culture, music, dancing, waterfalls, clear seas, horses, drumming and plenty of beautiful people to dance with. All day and night, my ears can feast on live salsa, Rhumba and folkloric grooves. Tonight, it is all perfectly poised underneath a big glowing moon, more charming than anyplace I have ever been. I am in love with this place. It is a world where the music never stops. Here, history still sings with passion through the eternal haunting choirs and hypnotic rhythms of a rich African heritage. I have discovered the pueblo of Trinidad in the province of Sancti Spíritus.

Trinidad was founded on December 23, 1514 by Diego Velázquez de Cuéllar under the name *Villa de la Santísima Trinidad*. Trinidad is one of the best preserved cities in the Caribbean from the time when the sugar trade was the main industry in the region. Trinidad's primary industries are tourism and tobacco processing. The historic district is well-preserved. It is maintained by the Cuban government to draw in and benefit from tour groups. In contrast, outside of the tourist areas, many homes are very run down and in disrepair, yet somehow still majestically beautiful. Tourism is the major source of income in the city.

Even before entering the gates of Trinidad's colonial majesty, I could feel that this place would capture my heart. The drive from Havana took me from the city into pueblos through a beautiful landscape of rolling green mountains and sensual swaying palms. We drove past dazzling vistas of the sea in bocas that open from the roadside into the vastness of the Caribbean. Entering Trinidad, I discovered a village with colorful pastel colonial buildings, cobblestone streets, and a world of music, mystery and dancing to explore, all framed between the ocean and the mountains. It fits my idea of heaven on earth perfectly.

I already know that, for this trip at least, I do not need to go any farther. Trinidad[8] is the place I have been hoping to find. I feel at home here.

The cobblestone ground beneath my feet is a challenge to turn on in the dance, yet I find myself loving the challenge. The speed of the dance gives me no time for mistakes. I wonder how I am going to not break an ankle tonight. I am at Casa de Música, an outside patio with cascading stairs that enter into a square colonial park named *Plaza Mayor* in Trinidad, Cuba. Dancing here is going to teach me a whole new world of possibilities in my body.

---

8   Trinidad lives together with the nearby Valle de los Ingenios. It has been a UNESCO World Heritage site since 1988. It is one of the best-preserved sugar trade cities in the Caribbean, and offers the best of everything one could want in Cuba. There are beautiful cascading waterfalls, clear azure seas with long stretching beaches, rolling green mountains and Cuban traditional music of all kinds that never stops. It is an idyllic picturesque colonial city with a rich history and kaleidoscope of cultural influences and amazing talented musicians and artists. For me, as a musician, artist, and nature lover, it offers everything I would want to have near me in one locale.

The night goes into hour upon hour of bliss-maximizing body rolling. I get very little chance to rest in between dances, which suits me quite fine. Scores of bodies twirl and spin in time to the music granting us a shared access to collective joy. I know no one here, yet I feel like I am with good friends and family. When the band finishes, the nightclub behind the main patio opens as a late night reggaeton dance hall. A short walk upstairs and the patio spills into a little courtyard that then steps down into a dark sanctuary of sensual Cuban reggaeton. A playground for sinful explorations if desired, but mostly a place to get a deep delicious groove on, surrounded by lovers of the dance. The room is an ancient roofless structure. The moonlight cascades in to bathe the dancers in soft glowing light. Trailing, tangled vines reach across the walls climbing up into the night air. Smoke billows up from countless cigarettes. Laughter echoes against the crumbling walls, creating a mystical ambiance that seems to celebrate the decay of all structure and form. Tables and chairs are strewn randomly around the perimeter and almost every other inch of space is filled with dancing bodies tightly packed together. I love everything about it. The energy is so sweet, so sensual, and so safe.

Late in the night on my way out the door, a man with tiny little braids takes my hand and invites me to dance. Of course, I am not eager to leave when I can dance more, so I accept. He pulls me in close to him. Our bodies move together as one. As we dance, he fills my ears with sweet incantations, professing his attraction to me, and how happy he is that he found me here. He tells me he's been watching me dance all night and that he wants to get to know me. Much to my surprise, he speaks perfect English. His name is Alexander.

We danced until the music stopped. He offered to walk me to my room and I accepted. The walk home on cobblestone streets was magical. Many others were also leaving, and the streets were filled with laughter and loud boisterous Cubans calling out to each other. Everyone walks home from the clubs in Trinidad. The pueblo is small enough, and most taxis aren't running at those hours anyway. The late nights after the dances end are some of the most fun times to be out with the people. Alexander walks me home slowly, asking me lots of questions about my life in the USA. At the door, he gives me the customary Cuban kiss on the cheek, then turns to leave.

As I start to put the key in the door, he turns and says to me, "Tomorrow, if you'd like, I would love to show you my city. I am an artist, and I would like to show you my paintings. I think you will like them very much." His sincerity is beautiful.

"That sounds lovely. I'll see you tomorrow then." I respond, touched by his good manners, perfect English and invitation to learn more about his world.

With a smile on my face thinking only of the moment of now, I drift into the dreamtime content.

Glimpses In: The Artist's Home

Alexander arrives exactly on time. He is tender, sweet, caring, sensitive and all mine if I were to want him. Unfortunately for him, I do not. He is a nice guy, but it is more than clear to me that he is to always remain in the "friend" or "brother" category for me. The chemistry simply is not there for anything more than that. However, the fact that he speaks English is very helpful for me, and since I am anxious to learn more about Cuba and Trinidad's unique culture, I was happy to accept his invitation to spend the afternoon together getting to know Trinidad more.

As we walk the bumpy cobblestone streets of Trinidad, he shows me the many galleries where his art is displayed. He is an incredible artist, and truly talented. I am in awe of his work. When he tells me what he sells them for, my jaw drops. I feel sad, but I do not say a word. Artists everywhere in the world are mostly undervalued, underpaid and struggling, but the price that he sells his work for is so low that I cannot imagine how he can even remain inspired to create and sell.

Yet, in Cuba, to make $20 off a painting, it is worth every minute he spends painting these masterpieces. I ask him how long it normally takes him to do a painting. "It depends, but normally about three days." Considering that many people here make $20 or less for an entire month of work, $20 for a three day project for him is a good income potential and potentially better than a government job if he sells them consistently. The problem, however, is that too many of his pieces are still hanging on the walls of the galleries around Trinidad and have not yet sold. There are scores of art galleries here. Even with a steady stream of tourists, it can be hard to know if his art is being shown, hung or even seen by potential buyers.

As we stroll through town, he tries to hold my hand several times. While endearing, I'm not accustomed to this and I feel a little bit awkward. Things move quick here in Cuba apparently. I have known him for less than twenty-four hours and he seems to be already thinking that we are a couple. He introduces me to his friends and family as his "novia." Everyone makes a point of telling me that he is a "Muy bueno hombre." I know they aren't lying. I can feel his sincerity and tenderness but I have no interest in being his, or anyone else's, girlfriend at the moment. I am amused that I have become his novia without any consideration whatsoever that I may not actually be interested in that title at all.

After the fourth time he presents me as his girlfriend, I decide to address it. "Alexander, I do not want you to be confused. I am not your girlfriend and I do not want to be introduced as your girlfriend. I am not looking for a boyfriend here. I am happy to be your friend, but nothing more." I tell him as matter-of-factly as possible.

My concerns are completely invalidated by his response. "This is how we do in Cuba. Little boys and girls, even ten years old: holding hands, novia and novio. It is normal here, do not worry," he says. I realize he missed my point, but chalk one up to cultural distinctions and let it go.

I can see that he is imagining falling in love with hopes that I am his ticket out of Cuba. I am tired, thirsty and hungry. He has invited me to his home for dinner so that I can see where he lives and meet his mother. It sounds like a great opportunity to get a glimpse into a real Cuban home here, so I accept. I make the mistake of assuming he lives around the corner when he says he lives "close by." When I find myself in a taxi with him that is driving us out of town farther and farther, I begin to worry. I really do not know him well at all. Lots of crazy thoughts run through my mind. I silently pray that he really is the good guy he seems to be and not some kidnapper or thug taking me to be robbed or killed for the $30 in my bag. Somehow I feel safe in spite of the wild ride my mind entertains me with. Thirty minutes after leaving Trinidad, the taxi finally stops. The sun has set, and it's getting dark quickly.

We exit the taxi and walk several blocks past concrete homes with a few Cubans strolling around, until we get to the end of a dark street.

"This is my house," he says proudly.

To my eyes, it is the least *house* looking house on the whole block. It looks more like an abandoned shed than a home from the outside. The low, cracked concrete walls are covered by a tin roof. It is dark and almost scary as night sinks in. For a moment my cultural conditioning passes through my mind. I feel anxiety knocking. I would never do this in my country, so why do I feel so safe to do it here? I know he is safe and pure of heart, so I gently bid the anxiety farewell and enter the house with him. The lights in the living room are not working. His mother is in the kitchen working.

For the outward appearance being what it is, the place is not dirty inside at all. To the contrary, it is actually quite clean. It is kept as well as it possibly could be for a mother and her son who make probably less than $20 a month combined. The concrete walls are splotchy. The paint is peeling and cracked. There are no water fixtures on any of the sinks, nor is there a visible shower in the bathroom of any kind. I wonder where they shower, or wash their hands. I silently pray I do not get sick eating here. I let go and trust that all will be OK.

He is proud of his house and his mother. There is no shame of any kind. I have noticed that in Cuba, there is not the same kind of relationship to what we call poverty, as there is in the USA. The fact is that the majority of Cubans live like this. Still, they are always proud to share, and they will warmly welcome people into their humble homes, no matter what condition the home is in. The Cuban people seem to have a strong sense of pride, and respect for themselves. No matter how things might appear on the outside, there is an inner dignity and strength in them that overcomes all deficits in the material plane. That dignity and pride does not succumb to the kind of shame or embarrassment that might exist in other cultures, especially my own.

Alexander is sweet, soft spoken, loving, and kind. I wonder if he can feel my anxiety and concerns in spite of my attempts to hide them. This is a world away from Trinidad's tourist center, and such a stark contrast to the world I come from. I don't really know where I am, or how to get back. I am totally dependent on him and in a place where I know no one.

"Come," he says, "I want to show you something. He pulls a piece of art off the wall and shows it to me. We have to go into the bedroom to look at it because the living room is far too dark. The painting portrays a rich intricate green jungle with a waterfall cascading through the center of it. It feels like some sort of vision of magic. There are glowing spheres hovering around the river's edge and floating through the waterfall. The jungle feels alive like it is popping off the canvas awakening in me.

"It is like a dream," I say to him.

He takes a step back and looks at me incredulously.

"You," he says, "are the first person who has ever seen that. That is what the floating bubbles represent is the dream. It is my symbol in many of my paintings." He was touched by my perception and understanding of his work and I could tell it enamored me more to him.

His mother serves me a huge plate of black beans with white rice, a plate of tomatoes and fried sweet potatoes. The food is delicious. I am starving and grateful to eat. Instantly I feel better and more relaxed. I had not eaten all day. Often in Cuba, I find that I go for many more hours without food than I am accustomed to. It can be hard to find the food I want to eat, when I want it, and there are not a lot of stores or places to purchase snacks. The snacks that are here are not snacks I really want to put into my body on a regular basis either. As a result, often I just do not eat until I am able to find real food.

This is life in Cuba. I am not alone in this. Everyone here has gotten accustomed to living this way. Some days there are eggs, many days there are not. Some days, one can find fruit, and many days one cannot. Some days they can afford meat, and many days they cannot even buy it if they have the money because there isn't any available.

After dinner we rearrange the tiny living room to dance to music played through the TV. The big heavy wooden government-issued rocking chairs are obstacles that have to be moved to make space for us to move. Alexander, like many Cubans, is a competent dancer. For an hour I am swirled, twirled and tossed through the 4x4 living room. I am tired yet so happy to be dancing. Finally, I have managed to leave all my bitchy western conditioning behind to just enjoy the present moment for what it is. His mother sits in a rocking chair, watching us, cheering and proclaiming, "Eso," when I make a move she likes. I am touched by the tender simplicity of this humble scene.

I cannot help but think of what will be lost in this culture when wifi, computers and cell phones take hold of households. At the same time, I cannot help but wonder what a normal night here is like for them, when there is not a guest to entertain. There is no TV, no computer, barely any light and no food in the refrigerator to munch on when they get bored. There is nothing to read and not enough light to read, even if you found a book. There is nothing to distract you from those who are there with you. Sitting, talking, making art or dancing is about all there is to do. I imagine they must sometimes feel the oppressive boredom of the mundane aspects of life, but I hope they never lose touch with their creativity and way of being together when they are bombarded by technoculture's illusions.

Taking a break from the dance, I notice the time. Sitting on the couch, Alexander professes his devotion to me once again.

"When I am with you, I want you to know you are safe. I want you to feel like you are with me. That is why I took you today to meet my most intimate friends and family. I want you to feel like we are a couple." He leans forward to kiss me.

I gently push him away. While he is attractive, sweet and kind, I still do not want to get involved with him in any kind of romantic way. I am not at all interested in being his girlfriend nor in being a couple. I graciously and clearly explain this to him again. Luckily, he is very understanding and not at all pushy.

When I ask him to, he walks me to the road where we find a taxi. A bright red '54 Thunderbird is my ride home. As it roars across the pavement back towards Trinidad, I close my eyes and rest. Reflecting on my day, I feel grateful for this glimpse into the reality of Cuba, away from the tourist traps. It is this tender natural humility that first captured my heart on this island nation that floats ninety miles away from my home state in the crystal blues of the Caribbean.

Rhythms of The Saints

The Religion is a rich, impenetrable mystery to me.
It is filled with magic, music and ancient spirits
that drift through the dances and songs taking me on journeys
into worlds long past and yet to come.

*T*he *strong, clear* rhythms of the drums sing out from behind a red brick wall interrupted by a metal makeshift door. The man behind the metal door moves aside as I enter with one of my teachers, Alexi. Alexi is an elder. He is hardened by his years of life in Cuba, but his heart is tender and true. His scruffy eyebrows are always expressive with wild unkempt tufts of grey. He always accompanies Alejandro, who is my primary drum instructor, for my classes and the Santería ceremonies I attend regularly with them. Alexi is Alejandro's uncle. As an elder, he is respected and honored. His hands are rough and strong from decades of drumming. He is reserved and quiet, but powerful. At nearly seventy-five years old, his yellowing eyes and rock hard belly show the signs of a lifetime of daily rum drinking. He is my *abuela:* my grandfather spirit here, a protector, a friend and a teacher. I have a very difficult time understanding his Cuban Spanish. He speaks quickly and with a sharp tongue, but I have come to learn he is almost always jesting even when he sounds serious. We have learned to communicate more in body language and energy than in words. Alexi is almost always drinking rum in a plastic cup. He never smokes and is always with his wits about him.

I met Alejandro and Alexi on my first day in Trinidad while taking a stroll from my casa to a cafe, near one of the small parks of the city. I heard Alejandro long before I saw him. From a distance, the drums called to me. The 6/8 bell part echoed across the cobblestone and drew me in from blocks away. Alejandro's drum spoke clearly above all the other drums. The inflections and syncopations of what he was playing were so familiar, so powerful and so enrapturing, that before I even saw him I knew I wanted to study with the man behind that sound.

By the time I made my way to where the drumming was coming from, they had stopped playing. All the musicians were lingering outside of the house where they had been holding an informal Santería ceremony. Alexi saw me watching and waved me over with a smile. I asked him who had been playing lead. He hobbled over to a short, almost bald, slightly chubby, baby faced man of maybe thirty years old with a gold tooth. Neither of them spoke a word of English, but I was able to convey that I wanted to study the religion and the drum.

I let them know that I had already done some preliminary work in Cojimar and wanted to continue here. His name was Alejandro. He agreed to teach me and invited me to attend ceremony with him to start our journey together. From that day on, I shadowed Alejandro any opportunity I got.

Entering the house, Alexi and I walk past the red brick wall, and towards a small concrete room, maybe eight by eight, with cracked paint and the pungent smell of mold drifting out from it. This is where today's *ceremonia de Santo* will begin. There are both a man and a woman *making the saint* today. The woman is dressed in red, representing Chango[9], and the man is dressed in blue to represent Yemalla[10]. Both stand unceremoniously waiting together. I cannot help but take note of the interesting role reversal of a woman being crowned by Chango and a man by Yemalla. In the tradition, however, it is not at all unusual. Many women are crowned by male Orishas, and many men guided by female Orishas.

The rhythms and songs are powerful. In the small space the sound is amplified, bouncing off the walls in loud cacophonous reverberations. Alejandro is playing a drum with two heads, and bells jingling off the side, commonly referred to in Cuba as *bata*. The *bata* are a family of three double-headed, tapered cylinders, with a slight hourglass shape. With varying sizes that produce differences in pitch, they are named according to size: *iyá,* is the largest drum, considered

---

9   Chango is the God of thunder and lightning. He is a warrior, his color is red and he carries an ax with him as his tool as he is also a farmer. He is known as the most promiscuous of the Orishas and had affairs with many of the female Orishas. He is fierce, loyal and a force to be reckoned with. He is also renowned for his pride and valor.

10   Yemalla is the mother of all Orishas and the goddess of the oceans in the Yoruba Religion. It was she who gave birth to the other Yoruba gods and goddesses. She is often syncretized with Virgin Mary figures of the Catholic Church, a practice that emerged during the era of the Trans-Atlantic slave trade. Her colors are blue and white. Yemalla is motherly and strongly protective. She does not easily lose her temper, but when angered she can be quite destructive and violent. She is associated with the moon, water, and feminine mysteries. She is the protector of women and governs everything pertaining to women; childbirth, conception, parenting, child safety, love, and healing.

the mother; *itótele,* is the medium size drum, and *okónkolo,* is the smallest or baby drum.

In this grouping the lead drum is actually the largest drum which also has the deepest sound (bass). The lead drum accents for the dancers, while the two smaller drums hold interlocking 6/8 patterns that create an incredible orchestra of rhythm and melody together. Bata is the traditional instrument of Santería ceremony. The conga parts often seen in *bembes* (fiestas/community events) were later employed with adaptations created that expanded the music of the Santería songs.

Alejandro is leading the songs and commanding the energy of the space with each slap and strike he makes. He motions for me to enter when he sees me peering in through the barred windows. He puts me in the corner, right behind one of the other drummers where he can guide me and keep an eye on me at the same time. The room is packed full of glistening bodies, mostly men. It is incredibly hot. Everyone is drenched and dripping with sweat.

The Religion is a rich, impenetrable mystery to me. It is filled with magic, music and ancient spirits that drift through the dances and songs. I feel so honored to have this kind of access to something that is often very hard to access if you are an outsider. I know that there are many things I may not ever be able to fully understand that happen in this world. Many of the ancient secrets of Santería are highly guarded and protected. Probably equally as many, or more, have been lost forever.

Alexi and Alejandro have shared with me during our lessons that fewer and fewer of the young people today are learning the traditions. When I ask them if the culture is being lost, they assure me that it will never be totally lost, but that maybe one day people will forget what it all means and why they do it. They tell me that in today's world, the reality is that very few of the practitioners themselves fully understand the Religion they practice. Yet somehow, the mysteries still live on, breathing through us all within the music and songs. They are intangible lingerings of an ancient theology that can never be understood intellectually. The realm of the spiritual is like this.

The drummers are mostly younger men with the exception of Alexi who is in his seventies and Chiquito, another elder whose age is impossible to guess. He could be fifty or he could be eighty. Chiquito is short, wiry, and missing most of his teeth. His crinkly black skin looks leathery and tired. He is stern and rarely smiles, but when he does, he lights up the world. He is small, but still a force to reckon with at all of five feet five. He and Alejandro are the leads in the ceremony, trading off singing, competing in moments, and always pushing the energy to its heights. They are so attentive to details in the music, and constantly correcting the energy when the younger drummers make a mistake or get distracted. I am witness to masters teaching new masters in the moments shared in rhythm.

The energy of the drums is hot, fast and super intense. I want to close my eyes and go into trance. Instead, I keep them open and watch, staying aware of the energy as it moves through the room. I know I am safe. I want to witness as much as I can to learn more of this mysterious religion.

A pregnant woman in the corner tries to leave the hot, stagnant room. On her way out, she collapses at the door, likely from heat exhaustion. I send out a silent prayer that she is OK and that she did not crack her head open on the concrete floors. Immediately, several men are with her, getting her up and helping her to find a place to sit. Two women come and stand next to her fanning her from both sides. I am grateful that she seems to be OK. The music never stops for a second. Most people ignore her and barely seem to notice that she collapsed.

A bucket of water is placed by my feet. No words are exchanged. I take initiative naturally, and watch for who needs water. I offer cups to the drummers in turn. It is a simple way I can be part of supporting the ceremony. In this simple action of service, a connection is established instantly. I am now a part of the family.

The opening to the ceremony ends quite unceremoniously. Everyone exits the tiny room sweating profusely and wiping their foreheads with white cloths or their T-shirts, chatting normally. Outside, the drummers take a short break, smoke, drink rum, and then reorganize for another round. As the second round begins, two men are almost instantly taken into trance, eyes closed with their bodies flailing about wildly in the small space. Instinctively, I move in closer to the drummers, to anchor the vacant space. I help to hold the rhythmical container by my presence, my clapping and the strength of my body. I am ready if either of the men falls into me or to any of the other musicians. I notice that a few of the drummers are watching me. There is a silent understanding passed between our eyes.

In the next break one of them calls me over and gives me a shot of rum. I know that in this way, I am being welcomed into their world. I take the rum with gratitude. It is as if he is saying, "I see you, and together we are doing this." We share a brief head nod and acknowledge each other with a slight bow and a touch of our hands to our heart. A symbol that is universal in the world of drummers, a sign of respect and love shared between us that needs no explanation. Wordless, but crystal clear, our communication is powerful in its silence. This is the world we share as musicians, and spirit workers.

The music starts again. Round after round, we share in the rhythms of the saints. Chants to the Orishas, dances, possessions, trances, flailing bodies and collapsing forms are all part of it. It is not glamorous or ego based in any way. The musicians are there as servants to the spirit world and no matter how wild it gets, or how many people collapse, no one backs down. The rhythms keep pounding through us; we ride it all the way through together. The spirits are in control of it all. The music never stops until the song is complete and every person there is transformed through sweat, soul and the spirits moving through us.

On the way back to my place, Alexi and I talk about Santería. I ask him questions, and try to understand his responses the best I can. His Spanish is very difficult for me to understand, and I think he is at least partially drunk which does not help. What I learn from him, I learn in the mannerisms, the energy, and in those moments where words are irrelevant anyway. I love this big gentle drunk grandpa of rhythm. I know he will be my friend for life.

I have a new family here in Trinidad. Once again, the ceremony and the interest in Santería are the gateways to being invited into another world here beyond the tourist facade. I have again found a world that is very much my domain. A place I feel more comfortable than any other: a world of magic, music, spirit, rhythm, song and altered states of being. A world I know as home: dancing and healing in the Rhythms of the Saints.

Two Boys for Every Girl

Her big, brown, painted eyes sparkle as she talks. Curly, dark hair frames her young face and drops down over her bare shoulders. She is dressed for the club in a short black mini dress and black Converse sneakers, Cubana style. Her painted lips part to hit her cigarette from time to time as she chatters away to me in perfect English.

"I lived in Europe before. I came home. Europe is not for me. I lived in Spain. I was very lonely there, but then some Cuban people found me and we would eat together at their home, and they helped me to make it. But really, I tell you, I missed Cuba too much. Listen, really Cheri, I love Cuba. There, the people, they work too much. It is miserable. No one is happy. They only care about money. I was so lonely there. I missed my family too much, and so I came home. I am happier here. Maybe someday I go back, but for now, I prefer Cuba. I am happier with my family and friends here. So we don't have so many things, but we have each other," she says and hits her cigarette again.

Christina has become one of my closest friends here in Trinidad. We meet almost every day now for conversation, laughs, and dancing all night long, drifting from one club to the next together as sisters. I appreciate everything about her. She is young, sassy, strong, clear, and solid in her independence as a woman. She loves to share stories with me of her travels in Spain, and more so I think she loves to practice her English.

Christina is well-educated. Her story is not unfamiliar to me anymore. For all of the Cubans who can't wait to leave, there are many who are happy to return home. I have heard similar reflections from many Cubans here who have left and then chose to return. They return for their family, their culture and their community that Europe and the USA just do not have.

I get it. I have lived in the USA most of my life. It was once the land of opportunity, but it seems to me now that it is quickly becoming a sinking ship, overburdened by technology and greed. Every time I think about having to return, and leaving Cuba, my heart sinks. If I allow myself to start thinking of going back, I feel utterly depressed and empty. It seems crazy, but I can see myself living here amongst these humble tender-hearted people and someday choosing to stay. The life here is sweet, natural and organic in such a different way. Of course, there are also serious problems and challenges here that most Americans would not be at all interested in dealing with, and that many Cubans resent. Most people here do not have a lot of money or material possessions. Certainly, they do not have the same access to opportunities or material things that we have in the USA. There are very deep economic and social problems that make life difficult for Cubans in ways that are unjust and troubling. Yet, what they do have is a kind of personal physical security that we can never even begin to understand. The cultural infrastructure, and the basics that the system does provide with health care, rations (albeit insufficient), and public services give them just enough to be able to survive, but certainly not enough to be able to thrive. There are no guns and the overall mentality of the culture is not one of violence, but instead one of cooperation and harmony. This too grants them a kind of personal safety that most of us in the USA will never have.

They also have the gift of time. They have time to invest in their art, and in their relationships. It is not the constant rat race of always striving to be successful and productive in every moment that the USA exists in. The mentality here is one of enjoying the moments for what they offer, and sharing what you have when you have it with whomever is there and/or in need. It is a more natural way of being in life. There is no success other than living a good life and sharing it with people you love. Life is not glamorous. No one here is trying to prove anything to anyone. There is absolutely nothing special about any of it. Ironically, that is what makes Cuba so special. It is so incredibly ordinary. Yet somehow, out of the ordinary comes the most extraordinary creations of community spirit, music, song and dance. I understand Christina's point too well.

Throughout this trip, I have been interviewing as many people as I can with a few simple questions to learn more about the values and concerns of the average Cuban. When asked what the three most important aspects of their culture are, so far 100 percent of Cuban's have included music, dance, community and family as their top priorities. Clearly music and dance are a priority here. It keeps them alive and helps them return to feeling happy in spite of challenging situations and confusing politics. In the music, they can forget their stresses and come together to celebrate life.

I have also been asking people how they feel they are being impacted by modern culture and technology. Surprisingly most of them have said that they do not see much of an impact at all.[11]

Sadly, I know that in five or ten years when I ask that question there will be a very different answer. They do not know yet what is coming. They are like innocent eager children wanting the sweet candy that will rot them from the inside out in time.

Christina and I go for coffee in one of the sweetest restaurants I have seen anywhere. Solananda is a large colonial home perfectly decorated with original antiques and European flair. The décor is tasteful and beautifully done, so much so that the restaurant won

---

11   The year was 2012 for this reference. More widespread use of Wifi did not come to Cuba until 2014/2015. In 2018-2020, when I asked some of the same people, they reported that technology is now disconnecting them. They reported that they miss people stopping by, because now everyone texts or calls. They reported also feeling more depression and disconnection because so many people are distracted by their phones. The youth and artists are now spending more time online than they are practicing their arts and the cultural arts are being lost to reggaeton and modern music. Modern culture is now affecting the culture much more than in 2012 when this story was written.

a contest in Europe for its design. It is located right in the heart of Trinidad close to Plaza Mayor. At the heart of the restaurant, there is an exquisite fountain and luscious tropical plants are strewn everywhere along the walls.

We sip coffee together from tiny, porcelain espresso cups. Christina gives me a discourse on men and relationships. She speaks with me in English so that her boyfriend, who is also with us, cannot understand her.

"I do not stay long in relationships. In the winter months, I like having one, because it is cold. When winter goes, I prefer single."

Her boyfriend stares through her. I wonder how their dynamic works. She is sassy, wild and full of life. He is quiet and reserved. Clearly she is in control and from the sounds of it, she uses men to give her what she wants, when she wants it and discards them when she is no longer interested. It seems cold, callous and borderline abusive, but she seems fine with it. In fact, I would say she is proud of it. She is one of the very few women here who have turned the tables on the men. Rather than being subjected to their control, she chooses men who she can use as she wishes, and leave when she pleases. I wonder if he understands more than she thinks. She insists that he does not understand one word of English.

"If he is ever jealous, even once, I am gone. I do not like it. I will forget him and move on tomorrow, because you know, if one is not good, there is always another waiting and always he will be better."

I think of my recent experience with Carlos. She is right, really. Her logic is well founded. There is no reason to cry or be sad over something that is not working well for you. If it works, it works. If it does not, the best thing is to cut your losses and move on without wasting time or energy trying to make something be what it is not, and most likely never will be. She is a good inspiration and reminder to me. I take notes mentally from this young woman, nearly 15 years my junior.

"In Cuba," she continues her monologue, "we like to fuck. Everyone does. Married or not, everyone has a girlfriend or a boyfriend on the side. No one cares. Sex is fun. I know many women who have a boyfriend and a girlfriend both. Here it is normal." She leans over and kisses her boyfriend, waves at the waiter for the check and pays for the coffee, then looks at me and says, "Dale, let's go dance, then I want to go home and fuck him all night." She laughs as she leans over and kisses her boyfriend passionately. I find myself in love with this young woman's spirit.

After our coffee, we make our way to the patio of Casa de Música to enjoy another delightful night of dancing and music together. The dance floor is packed already with sweaty bodies spinning tirelessly in perfect time to the music. The moon is big, full and bright. It shines down on us in its quiet dance across the sky. I've found my own little Shangri-La in Cuba. A moonlight patio, dancing all night long to world-class music, and feeling life and music live through me while being spun around all night by countless sexy men who really know how to dance: this is my idea of heaven.

On the dance floor, a smiling Cuban man with little dreadlocks is pushed into me by a voluptuous Cuban woman dressed in yellow. I resist for a moment, but surrender instantly when he takes my hand and I feel the way he moves. We are a perfect match. Our energies become one instantly. We are fire feeding fire. We take salsa to the edge of super funkification and then back in a long dance that has us both laughing out loud with smiles plastered on our faces. Everywhere I look around me, as he spins me around, I see smiling faces and happy glowing people dancing and celebrating life.

At the end of the dance, he hugs me hard with great enthusiasm, his sweaty cheeks rubbing against mine. He tells me his name is Jorge. He is a big-eyed, strong-bodied man, perfectly sculpted from head to toe, with a smile that takes up his whole face.

Christina comes up behind me smiling and says, "Wow, you gonna dance like that all night? You are incredible. Now, watch me dance with him." And I do. I thoroughly enjoy watching my two new friends dance to the music they have been raised with. I laugh with them as they spin and shake their bodies together in bliss. Even with hundreds of other people around, the three of us have our own little world together.

My mind is free of all other thoughts. I am totally content and granted total permission to simply be myself here, fully and shamelessly expressed in my passions of music and dance. I know I will see Jorge again as he walks down the stairs to meet his friends who are waiting. I adore him from afar hearing his boisterous laughter exploding through the night as he greets them. He is pure light and love in form. Every part of his being is rhythm in motion.

Later, Christina and I found our way to La Cueva, or Disco Alaya as it is formally named. The journey to the cave is dreamlike and its own special experience. Walking on broken cobblestone streets with flowing water making little riverlets, passing homes that are quiet at midnight while feeling the coolness of the mountain night air makes it a magical late night walk.

Disco Alaya is a Trinidad favorite. It is a nightclub created inside of a cave. When I heard about it, I had no idea what to expect. I envisioned a small opening into a short cave with a speaker and a DJ. To my surprise, when I entered the first time, I discovered that it is much more than I could have imagined. The cave has a huge dance floor and is truly its own underground world of body bumping fun. Water drips non stop from the ceiling making the tile floors muddy and slippery and the rum and rhythm mixes until 3 am. This is another world here in Trinidad. It's a world that instantly intrigues and captivates me for its raw, primal, animalistic booty shaking yumminess. The place is packed. The energy is thick with the primal, sexual sensuality that makes Cuba so addictive.

Walking onto the dance floor with Christina leading me, my hand in hers, I see a man whose physical beauty stuns me. He is a giant of a man. Standing close to seven feet tall, with soft creamy brown skin, he towers over everyone else. He is intensely cool and aloof. I can feel his eyes on me, and a rise of anticipation surfaces in me. After a long gaze, he looks away when someone greets him. Christina is dancing like a wild child grinding her plump body round and round, getting the attention of as many boys as she can. When I look again, he is gone. I am almost relieved. A man that beautiful is dangerous for me.

Moments later, I see him return to his perch. Slowly, walking with intention and a strong gaze, he approaches me and reaches for my hand, and invites me off of the dance floor.

"De donde eres?" He asks me. (Where are you from?)

"Soy Americana," I say, instantly drawn into him and held firmly in his huge hand.

"I thought you were Cubana," he says to me in English. I laugh at the comment, one I have heard many times lately. I feel sure that I am going weak in the knees being this close to him. Something in me is touched by his tender way of speaking.

"You know Christina? I live in Europe, but I am from Trinidad. You want to sit down and talk with me?" he asks me. His soft voice and sincerity intrigue me. My heart is racing.

"Yes, but not here. It's too loud," is all I can manage. He keeps a hold on my hand and I invite him to a quieter spot in the club away from the dance floor where I can hear what he is saying. We sit at a table near the entrance. When my eyes fall on his face, I have a difficult time breathing. I am quite sure that I have never seen a man this exquisitely beautiful. I am overtaken with his physical perfection. I want to touch his face and feel his skin and taste his lips all at once. His eyes are shiny, playful and deep, all at the same time, with the most amazing, perfectly curled lashes. His hands are huge and strong and my hand in his makes me feel safe, protected, and held. He tells me a little bit of his story. I try to focus on his words but my mind is crazy with desire. I discover that it is hard to focus with the rum and the desire making for that dangerous Cuban cocktail once again.

I can tell he is not the typical Cuban guy when he asks for my number and says "Good night. I will call you tomorrow," then leaves the club alone. His name is Fernando. I am sad when he leaves, but also a little glad to get back to the dancing with Christina. Red flags are waving wildly inside. All my wise woman warning systems are at full alert, and I can't wait to see him again.

Christina winks at me when I return and smiles. "Fernando is a very good man. He is different. He has respect." We dance til three in the morning and stumble down the hill, laughing the whole way down.

As I drift off to sleep, around 4 am, I find myself smiling and replaying moments of the night like a movie in my mind. Christina's sassy wildness, the cobblestone dance floor, the best dance of my life with Jorge, the feeling of the sweat pouring off my body, the euphoria in the music, the walk up to Disco Alaya over the muddy river of cobblestones, the drippings from the roof of the cave and the hot steamy bodies dancing in unison underground. I press pause when the image of Fernando comes to my mind and replay his soft voice and his tender curiosity over and over in my head. And from the Comedy Central channel in my brain I suddenly hear the melody of the song, "Surf City," by Brian Wilson and Jan Barry, where the lyrics sing "Two girls for every boy," playing in the background.

When in Cuba, do as Cubans do, so why not "Two boys for every girl?" I fall asleep smiling.

Amor

*T*he *night air* stirs as it wraps around me embracing me in a cool breath. My heart races to keep calm. The scent of his cologne washes across me and a calm powerful desire stirs deep in my being. I cuddle deep into the pocket of his arm and stare at the sky. I am content here. If time stopped at this moment, I would be quite OK with it.

"Cheri," his soft tender voice sings to me, "Tell me, Cheri, tell me, do you have other relations? You know, at home? Do you have a boyfriend? Cheri, tell me, I want to know." His broken English is somehow endearing. Sincerity oozes out of him. He is so big and strong and impressive in every way, yet when he speaks it is the softest most tender presence I've ever felt in a man.

I start to tell my story, deeply nestled into his chest. He stops me short.

"Hey, look at me when you talk. I want to see your eyes." I turned and met his eyes. I was already completely and dangerously in love with this man: fully head over heels.

His beauty overcomes me quickly. I am suddenly shy and girlish. I touch his face lightly and he kisses me before letting me go on. Truly, his is the most exquisite face I have ever laid eyes upon. As I speak, his big curly-lashed eyes drink in my story. I am swimming in the world of his eyes as my story comes pouring out of me. In moments I have to stop and take a breath or I'll be lost in his gaze forever.

For hours into the night, we share stories and talk. As the air got cooler, I cuddled deeper into him.

"What are you doing tomorrow? Would you want to go have dinner somewhere with me, maybe at a restaurant? Maybe we can go to the beach?" He said to me before he left.

How could any woman say no to that. "I would like that very much, Fernando," I said.

He kissed me goodnight; I felt respected and cherished in that moment. I watched him walk down the cobblestone street before returning to my room for the night, floating between the worlds, barely able to believe that I had spent the evening wrapped in the arms of the most beautiful man I had ever seen.

The next day, I had just arrived in the park when he pulled up riding a scooter, waving a helmet. It took me a second to realize it was him, but who else in this town is that big after all? A giant on a scooter waving a helmet at me has to be him. I kiss him on the lips when I see him.

"Are you hungry?" he says.

"Yes, I am starving." I respond. I was not expecting him to show up on a scooter. I feel the enthusiasm of a little girl, excited for a journey into the unknown with the most beautiful man on the planet. I hop on the scooter and we take off through the cobblestone streets of Trinidad out to the main road that leads to the beach.

I wrap around him from behind and feel the joy rising in my heart for the adventure that is my life right now. The cool air of the early evening is inviting on my face. He squeezes my thigh a few times as we ride.

I find myself giggling, "What?" he says to me in the wind of the ride.

"I'm so happy." I say and leave it there.

"Me too Cheri, I am very happy with you," he says as he turns his head to blow me a kiss in the wind.

Closing my eyes, I let the memories cascade through my mind's eye as the wind whips my hair around my face. I think of all of the amazing things that have transpired since I arrived in Cuba just a few short weeks ago. It feels like a lifetime in and of itself, like some amazing movie that I am the star of. All of my old life has lost relevance. All there is, is now, in this world called Cuba. It has consumed my life and made the life I left behind feel meaningless and empty in comparison. Life here is so tangible, so earthy, and real in every way. The beauty and the pain, the challenges and the joys, the life and the death of it are so tangible. Life is palpable. There is an intimacy with humanity that I have longed for but rarely experienced in my own country. I love it.

I can not explain it, but I am even more in love with this country than when I left last time. I really do not want to leave. The thought of leaving is too painful right now and stealing my bliss. I push it aside and bring my focus back to the night that is unfolding. I open my eyes surprised that we are turning into a neighborhood. I think he must be stopping to visit a friend on the way, but a few turns and a lot of bumps and puddles later, I see the glowing lights of a restaurant ahead of us. He parks the scooter, and we walk down a carefully lighted path with small lanterns on either side of the walkway and a string of low hanging lights above us. What I see is enchanting to the senses in every way.

I find myself standing next to him in an absolutely charming restaurant, with a beautiful garden spreading out around the tables. The place is uber romantic and magical, with little glimmering lights and candles sparkling everywhere. There are only two other couples there. I feel like a queen, with her king.

We talked over dinner about his life in Spain, about his family, and my family. He has to really listen to understand me, as his English is far from perfect, but it is good enough for me to understand him perfectly, even if he does not always understand me perfectly. He squints a little when he is listening hard, and I can tell he is really working hard to grasp every word I say. He is totally attentive and fully focused on every word I say.

"Que quieres? What do you want now?" he says, and once again I am touched by the way he wants to know my heart and feelings. He is so sincere.

"I want one good devoted man, a strong community and a good life filled with music, love and good friends. A simple life, peaceful and with enough money to live comfortably," I answer.

"I want to kiss you," he says and puts his face forward for me to meet. I put my hand on his face and kissed him sweetly.

He smiled a big beautiful smile and time stopped for those few seconds as our souls touched between the worlds.

"I like you very much, Cheri. Maybe I can be that one man for you. I want to try. Will you let me? Maybe you can come to Spain to be with me? Or maybe one day I can come to your country too." He says to me in total seriousness.

I am taken aback and do not know how to answer, and when the waiter comes with the check, I smile and leave the question unanswered in my awkwardness.

He already has his papers out of Cuba, he doesn't even live in Cuba anymore. Could this man actually be sincere? The question quiets me and I say very little the rest of the night. Something is triggered in me that has not been awakened in a very long time.

We hop back on the scooter and ride to the beach to watch the moon shimmer across the Caribbean. He holds me quietly and we rest together in each other's arms both lost in our own worlds of contemplation of what a life together might be like or if it could truly be possible.

Quiero Saber

"*Que piensas?* Quiero saber." he says to me with concern on his face, "tell me, please."

The truth is, in his presence, I do not want much else. When I am with him, he is all I want and all I can think of. His perfectly curled lashes frame his eyes and he looks at me with such sincerity and sweetness that I have a hard time speaking. What I want to say is that I just want to spend the rest of my life looking at him every day, but instead I say, "I just want a little time with you before you go."

Around us the world continues, but we are in our own world here sitting at a small table in a restaurant. I am weakened by his physical presence and by the tenderness in his voice. He seems so genuine, so sincere, so true right now. I do not know what to think. I only know that I savor these moments when we are alone together away from the streets and all the distractions of other people we both constantly have. The times alone are never long enough. In a few days he will depart for Spain to return to his life there, and soon after I will be leaving to return to my life in the USA.

"You want to continue relations with me after I leave? Tell me, seriously. This is serious. I need to know. What do you want? What do you think? At home in Spain, it is easier for me. I can Skype you, and email you, you know? What do you think?"

I can not even believe he has to ask, but I am glad that he does. I am happily surprised that he is thinking this way. I am touched by his sincerity. I know he can have any woman he wants, any time he wants. I am quite sure of that. I have seen the way women throw themselves at him, and how many female friends he has. I imagine many women would not have the strength to stand up to him in the ways that I have. He is an incredible force. We have had many disagreements and a few pretty intense fights over his jealousy and attempts to try to control me.

When he is sober, he is tender, kind, soft spoken and reasonable. Unfortunately, when he has been drinking rum, which seems to be just about every day, he becomes difficult, loud, controlling and excessively jealous. He nearly hit a guy on the stairs of Casa de Música one night just for saying hello to me, then blew up and made a huge scene over it, waving his big arms and talking so loud I had to just walk away from it all.

I have stood my ground and continued being who I am in his presence, and it has challenged him in every way imaginable. He does not like that I am a dancer and that I dance so freely with whom I choose. He does not like that I have so many male dance friends, yet he has equally as many (if not more), female friends that he talks with everywhere he goes. The double standard does not jibe with me very well. I have been very clear about expressing that. In short, I am the liberated independent American woman in stark contrast to the submissive woman he possibly wishes I would be for him. Yet somehow, the love keeps returning. We talk through it, he understands and acknowledges his issues and we try again. This gives me hope of a breakthrough that likely will never come.

"We can stay in touch, of course Fernando. I would like that very much." I kiss his forehead and he pulls me close in a big happy hug. I am not at all naive enough to think that he doesn't have a woman in Spain and probably one or two others here in Cuba. Staying in touch is safe and comfortable. Committing to be his girlfriend or partner is not even a consideration after what I have been through with him and his crazy making.

"I have to take my children now, I am coming back. I see you later OK?" He kisses me and takes my hand in his and says, "I am very happy that you want to continue with me. Maybe one day, we can have a house here and live together and be happy here in Cuba."

As he leaves, I think about the likelihood of that actually happening. He is on his way back to Spain soon. Soon after I will be on my way back to the United States, with no real idea on when or how I will come back to this crazy rock in the Caribbean. The romance of it is intriguing, and even exciting, yet the real potential is a very different thing. There is no doubt that I was head over heels in love with this man from the first moment I saw him. There is no doubt that I am more in love with him every time we have some quiet time together to share and talk quietly. My heart loves his tenderness and the way he engages with me when we are alone. The fact that we share a vision of having a home here makes me want to try to make it work.

On the other hand, there is nothing *but* doubt that this relationship could actually be sustainable or healthy for me in the long run. I have had enough doubt raised in two short weeks to know better than to get more involved. The wise woman in me is screaming RUN and never look back. He is stubborn, incredibly hotheaded, exceedingly jealous, and drinks rum most of the afternoon and night until he is so drunk he can barely stand up. He often does not show up when he says he will. When he gets drunk, he is absolutely impossible to talk to and his head is filled with stories similar to what I experienced with Carlos in Havana. Now, with one Cuban relationship behind me, and one simmering in front of my face, I know those red flags are *los dios* trying to tell me something. I know I should listen more carefully, yet nothing can change the love that I feel in spite of my wisdom that he could never be a good partner for me.

Some say love is blind. My experience is that love is not blind. Romance may be blind. Fantasy may be blind, but real love is the polar opposite. We are blinded by our own delusions of what love is. Love is not seeing someone for their potential and being disappointed when they do not reach that potential. That is the world of romance, fantasy, and, quite frankly, it is a bit delusional. True love is seeing someone as they truly are. It is appreciating that person exactly as they are without needing or wanting to change them in any way whatsoever. True love requests nothing in return and holds no expectations or grievances. True love is a thing that is beyond rare in this world.

It is actually more loving to let go of expectations, of false hopes and dreamy idealistic potentials and to love freely and fully. It is more loving (both to ourselves and to others) to simply be present with what is real, and not be attached to our own desires of what we wish it could be.

Cubans are very skilled at this way of being in life and in love. They are present to what is present. They accept each other and life as it is, for better or worse. They do not expect life to be anything but what it is. They live in a much more grounded understanding of relationships and life. Cubans know that relationships come and go. Here, in relationships, things move very quickly. Yet through it all, more often than not, lifetime friendships are grown and cultivated over time. There are no false dreamy hopes of Prince Charming or knights in silver armor coming to rescue the damsels in distress. Cuban relationships operate in the world of reality. Their lives are much more fluid as a result of this way of being. I have much to learn from their ways here. While some might see it as more coldhearted, I see it as just being real with the reality. If we spent even half as much energy just accepting people and things as they are, as we do in trying to change them, we might just find one of the secrets to long lasting peace and tranquility.

Ramblings and Reflections

Silence is a very rare thing in village life. It wakes me in the early morning moments from a deep sleep. I enjoy savoring its short-lived sweetness before the day begins. At 6 am, the first street vendor pierces the silence.

"Hay pan." His strong voice cracks the quietude and echoes through concrete corridors and cobblestone streets.

I love the calls of the street vendors and the rhythmical interplay with life that they create. His calls seem to be perfectly synchronized with the rooster, "Hay pan," a rooster call and then his call again. Every product sold in the streets has its own unique incantation, and its own rhythm. "Lechuga," rises on the 'chuga' syllable and reminds me to buy lettuce. "Habichuela" rolls the second syllable a little faster than the first, for green beans. "Cebolla, ajo" accentuates the last syllable and sometimes sounds like one word rather than two to my ears. One bread seller here has a whistle he blows several times before he shouts out "Hay pan." His rhythm is a little different than the others. There are several different types of breads sold in the street and each vendor's call differentiates his bread from the others. "Criolla pan," is large loaves of hard bread. "Pan suave," is soft bread, sometimes in loaves, and sometimes in small buns. It is always sold fresh and warm, just out of the oven, and it is always delicious.

The street vendors know their customers and their customers know them. Part of their work every day includes chatting with community members about daily life. I have watched them many times standing in doorways inquiring about the families, smiling and sharing the happenings of their lives as they sell their goods. There is this innate sense of connectivity in every aspect of life here. Everything is a song or a dance or a story in motion. Expression, song, rhythm and music are woven into the fabric of life in almost every minute.

In fact, if there was one word I could use to describe Cubans, it would be expressed. The irony of the fact that theirs is a political regime that does not encourage freedom of expression, especially around certain topics, does not elude me. Yet on a personal day-to-day basis, in their homes and communities, Cubans are highly expressive people in their mannerisms and ways of being. The drama of life is always alive in their expressions. They will cry easily when they are sad. They shout and throw tantrums when they are angry. They talk about their problems and love to discuss things from every perspective imaginable. They laugh and cut up together and are always in a conversation with someone any time they walk down the street. I love this way of familiarity that they have with each other. It is one of my greatest pleasures here to witness it and be a part of it every day.

A perfect example of this is happening right now where I am sitting. For the past hour the little girl downstairs has been screaming at the top of her lungs. No one seems to care much. No one tries to stop her. From what I can tell, she has total permission to be as loud and crazy as she wants to be, for as long as she desires and no one could care less. She is not scolded or coddled. She is just allowed to cry and rage until she is complete with it. Her family is there, and there is no lack of love or care, but they will let her go on until she is complete. It is simply culturally acceptable and no one is going to take away that child's right to throw her tantrum.

This kind of highly expressive behavior is accepted in Cuba without question. At all hours of the day and night, it is common to hear the sounds of wild tantrums from strong-willed children, who learn this behavior from parents who are very highly verbally expressed, fiery and strong-willed themselves. In the streets, you will constantly hear people hollering *"Oyeee,"* or *"Pipo"* down the streets to get the attention of someone. Loud voices and hard conversations are normal, and nothing is sugarcoated to try to protect anyone's feelings. I often think about how much effort is put into speaking with political correctness in the USA, especially in the spiritual communities I have been a part of. Being here, where everyone is just blatantly real and straightforward is actually refreshing for me. No one is trying to find the *right* way to say things, they just express themselves naturally and without filtering. If someone likes you, you will know. If they do not, you will know even faster and there is no beating around the bush to get to the heart of the issue.

There is rarely total silence in the pueblo. Even with the inherent tranquility of this place, it is a world of soundscapes filled with life in every moment. I enjoy listening to it. I find it comforting, warming and soothing, rather than annoying. It feels like I am part of a community here, even when I am alone in my bed. Just by being able to hear life happening, I am somehow connected to the life that moves through these streets. I rarely feel lonely or alone here. If I do, I just take a walk outside my casa, and I am instantly met with smiles and people who are willing to stop and listen to my heart if I want to share it. No one is too busy to care, and Cuban people love to engage in the art of conversation just for the simple pleasure of it.

Many days I do not think at all about my life back home. Many days I cannot imagine having to return. Most days I pray for a way to not have to. In comparison, life in the USA is isolated, cold, disconnected and quite lonely. The streets are almost always empty and quiet in many neighborhoods. People do not just hang out on the streets chatting or playing cards anymore in the typical American neighborhood. If they did, someone would surely call the police and report that there is suspicious behavior happening in their neighborhood. I feel alone and isolated almost always in my country, and the contrast is painfully evident in the way people treat each other. People in the modern world do not really want to be bothered too much, and are so busy they rarely have time to enjoy the art of conversation and simple sharing of humanity.

Of course, there are plenty of problems here. There is no such thing as a perfect place or a perfect system of government. Even with all that I love about Cuba, it is obvious that the system here has a lot of problems. The crippling lack of resources and economic instability are clearly two of the biggest problems. The incredible inflation for basic products combined with low to no pay cripples the people's spirits and offers them virtually nothing in the way of opportunities to advance their lives. Lack of access to information and current news is a concern here. Medicines and health care, while free, are often unavailable. While there is a lot of propaganda about health care and Cuban doctors being well-educated and world-renowned, the truth is that the hospitals and healthcare that the average Cuban gets access to is disturbingly inadequate. The international hospitals and clinics where tourists go are a step up from the Cuban hospitals, yet still a far cry from what we have become accustomed to in the USA and Europe in sanitation, technology and facilities.

Families and individuals, of course, have their own problems and dramas happening. Economic stress, domestic violence, rape, sexually transmitted diseases, dysfunctional families, and even murder: yes, it all happens here in Cuba just as it does anywhere else humans exist. In spite of their layers upon layers of problems, however, the Cuban people, for the most part, are more gregarious, relaxed and fulfilled here by their families and communities than most of the people I know in the USA. I cannot speak to whether they are happier or not as happiness is a fleeting thing that is there in a moment and gone in the next.

What I can attest to is that Cubans are highly adaptable and skilled at managing life. They know how to let things go and enjoy life and their families in spite of the seemingly unending challenges they face every day. They know how to love each other and make the best out of what may not be the most optimal situations. In spite of seeming impossibilities, the people somehow find it in their day to day life to enjoy each other, to sing, to dance, and to transform the sufferings of their lives into budding blossoms of love through an overriding acceptance of life as it is.

Still, there are many aspects of the system in Cuba that I think, at least in theory, had some intentions of trying to serve a higher sense of humanity, in spite of the painfully obvious problems. I cannot help but to think that the government was smart in some ways to restrict full access to certain parts of modern culture: specifically porn, extreme displays of violence in the media, and full, open, immediate access to cell phone technology, the internet and computers. Undoubtedly, now more access is needed for the country to be part of the world's evolution, and undoubtedly it is coming. However, experiencing what has happened to not only my own life and family, but to the whole of the USA and the world, with total freedom of access to everything imaginable under the sun, I cannot help but feel that Cuba has been wise in their choice to sit back and watch the impact technology is having on the rest of the world before opening the doors fully. I know that some of the people here really want full access, but I also know that not all of them do. The older generation knows the dangers lurking in the outside world can damage the innocence of their culture and the elders speak of cell phones and the internet addiction as "the sickness," or "*la enfermedad.*" Most young people have not yet considered what the full impact of technology and widespread open internet access will be to their culture, communities, families and individuals.

The fact that for many years, the government has controlled what the people have access to is obviously not ideal. However, it has maintained a certain cultural purity and system of values that most of the world has long since forgotten. I cannot help but be curious about the early visions of Fidel Castro, and his ability to somehow see what perhaps many others could not. Perhaps in his earlier years, he subscribed to a belief that to protect something precious, you have to deny certain evils and external forces from infiltrating.

Cuba has very little of the type of crime we face every day in the USA. There is a day to day sense of security and a tranquility here that speaks volumes of the impact that these hard-lined controls have created. No one in Cuba can even understand what it means to live in a culture where you are often fearful of any little sound at night, because someone may enter your home with a gun to rob or kill you. They do not know what it is like to fear someone attacking you in a parking lot, or shooting your child in a school. Most have no idea what it is like to feel afraid to walk anywhere alone, and especially at night, without fear of consequence. They have no understanding whatsoever of what it is like to live in an environment where at any moment you could become a target of some random psychopath's stray bullet in just about any place from a church to a grocery store, in your car or even in your own home.

Crime in Cuba has real consequences both from the police, and from the community. It is harder to get away with things in Cuba because there are always eyes watching, and life is so interconnected. There is also a strong social pressure to conform to certain norms. Those who do not are ostracized or heavily penalized to send a message to the rest that walking the straight and narrow path is the only real way to live well amongst others. There is little to no access to guns or weapons of mass destruction such as assault rifles and machine guns. An unarmed public may sound scary to hard-liners in my country, but it also prevents the kinds of things we have every day like school shootings and senseless killing sprees.

Cubans have a security system built into their community that works better than the police ever could. The fact that there are such strict laws and controls most certainly has had a long term impact on the way people treat each other. This sense of physical safety, security and familiarity allows people to be human together.

I am always interested in hearing from the Cuban people directly on how they feel about their culture and government. In listening to them speak, my fears around Cuba losing its cultural identity in the face of modern culture are calmed. The people here, in Trinidad at least, are committed and strong in their awareness of the value of their cultural identity. Perhaps Cuba has a chance of withstanding the onslaught of modern culture's malaise. Only time will tell. In my interviews and conversations with Cuban people, what I have been learning is that there is a very mixed energy on the island. Many people want change, and strangely enough, almost as many do not.

Many people see the scourge that modern culture has on the world, and they do not want to lose their country, their culture and their way of life to modern culture's insanity. These are often the ones who have friends and family members who have left Cuba and returned with stories of having to work too hard for too little money and of never having time to be with friends and family. These are the Cubans who, like my new friends, Fernando and Christina, have lived in Europe or the USA, and who came back to the island reporting on living empty, meaningless lives. Lives that were all about just working for money to constantly pay bills for things that in Cuba are often free or cost very little.

The younger generation, of course, wants the fast-paced life, the excitement, the cell phones, the computers and the options for more, yet many of them will say openly that they feel that Castro has done a lot of good things for Cuba. They want change, and yet they also truly love their country. A great number of them say that they love Castro in spite of the problems his regime has created for them. They are aware that there is no such thing as a perfect system and that by moving to another country, one only trades one kind of problems and stresses for another. The older ones, from my interviews, are loyal to Castro more often than not. They speak about the fact that while many of the problems they have encountered might have been created by their system, the problems they would have had without Castro, especially if the USA had maintained its stronghold here, would have been much more damaging to their culture, communities, and way of life. They are proud of the Revolution and a good 80 percent of them say they will fight to the death if the United States ever tries to take over Cuba. Equally as many say that they would vote for Castro in a free election, if they could.

Village Life

Horse hooves on cobblestone
Whispering palms
The sweet sound of children laughing in the street
A television chattering today's news in the distance
Flocks of well-trained pigeons cascade across the darkening sky
responding to the shrill whistles of their owners hovering
on scores of rooftops in the village as the rhythms of reggaeton
and sultry son drift across the soft cool breeze.
Yipping dogs, roosters and the cries of street vendors
making a last round on their way home
All merging to form the eternal, always present songs of the pueblo.

My heart is hurting already thinking of leaving this country in ten short days. I am so content here. I do not miss anyone or anything at all. I can not help but fantasize about not coming back and just disappearing quietly into the heart of Cuba. I find myself imagining meeting a Cuban with a beautiful home in Trinidad and marrying him, creating a life here and forgetting about the rat race forever.

I know that most any Cuban man would marry me in a moment for the opportunity to be able to leave. However, practically speaking, that fantasy is filled with challenges and difficulties. I know how most Cuban people live here would be very challenging for anyone from my culture to thrive in for long. The majority of Cuban homes lack efficient systems for things I am accustomed to. Things like running water and functioning plumbing are not the norm in the average Cuban home. Many of the homes are falling apart from the inside out. The paint is falling off, the beams are cracking and breaking, the smell of mold, piss and age are wafting through the ethers night and day. Most homes are old structures badly in need of renovations. Very few Cuban families have any resources whatsoever to be able to keep up with even the most basic of maintenance that a home requires to be in good condition. Often, in the outskirts, away from the tourist centers, they are homes similar to my artist friend, Alexander's, with a metal roof placed on top of a concrete foundation that is barely standing. I am amazed that they are able to endure so much rain, so many tropical storms and even hurricanes in these makeshift structures.

There are many other complications. As an American in Cuba, I cannot use a bank card, a credit card or even receive money via Western Union in my name. I have to send it to a Cuban national, and trust that person enough to make sure the money gets to me. It is almost impossible to own anything here, as an American, as far as property or a vehicle. Even with money, there are a lot of issues in getting the things you need. The stores have very low to no supplies of even the most basic things like dish soap, a blender or a water filter for example. Nothing here is at all like the USA, with all of our conveniences and access to basic day-to-day necessities. In time, I am sure it could become quite challenging. Equally, I can also see that in time, one would just accept, adapt and find solutions as needs arise. Cubans are very resourceful and creative, because every day there is a new challenge to work through.

The truth is that, for now at least, I am completely content here. I absolutely love being here. I enjoy the challenges. It is fun to hunt for things that I need, as it takes me into the community to connect and talk with others. I always discover something or someone along the way that makes the experience more interesting. Some days I wander all day looking for one small item. Along the way I run into friends and enjoy a social day. Usually someone points me in the right direction eventually, and almost always I find what I need in the most unexpected of places. The experience, while sometimes challenging, is not all bad by any means. It is the people I meet along the way that add richness to the hunting.

I love the sounds, the sights, the smells, the tangible presence of familiarity in the air. I love the music everywhere, and the backdrop of the constant murmur of families and street vendors selling their food walking through the barrios. All are welcomed parts of the orchestra of life here in this charming village. I honestly feel that I could live here for the rest of my life and never miss a thing about modern culture. I cannot connect whenever I want to the internet or wifi. I do not mind at all. It is a sanctuary of returning to the roots of humanity, returning to true presence and remembering the magic and mystery that is available in life when we are not always staring at screens and seeking the ever elusive dangling carrot on a stick of maybe *someday*, but instead just living in the moments of now because it is all there is to do.

Trinidad, undeniably, is a special place in Cuba. There are very few pueblos of this size that I could actually consider living in, as a foreigner, because of their lack of infrastructure and certain basic necessities for me. Things like bottled water, and products and services that cater to foreigners are easier to find here than in most places in

Cuba. Trinidad was named a UNESCO world heritage site in 1988 and as such it is and has been a very popular tourist destination for many years. The people here have more access to income potential than most places in Cuba because of that fact. Due to an almost constant exposure to foreigners, they also have a bit more of an expanded mentality than much of the rest of Cuba. The music and dance that I love here so much are all a part of what is provided to keep the tourists well entertained and culturally fed. Artists, musicians and dancers come from all over Cuba to work here. The roots of Trinidad's music extend back to the slave and sugar plantation era with the Africans who were brought here in the 18th century. The area is rich in its African heritage and the music and dance continues to evolve as its own form, specific to Trinidad.

The softness of the morning sun is starting to fade into the strength of day. The birds are still singing, but the sounds of life in the village are taking over. The gentleness of the morning is lost quickly here as strong, loud voices crash across the quietude that so rarely exists for more than a few moments in this village.

The day beckons me forth as Oya sends me a gentle breeze to inspire me into her magic again.

Two Boys for Every Girl: Part 2

n Cuba, it is common for men and women to have more than one lover, and more than one significant person in their lives. Many, if not most, Cubans, married or not, have auxiliary relationships outside of their primary relationships that last for years and often entire lifetimes. It is understood, and expected, and while few of them will openly discuss or admit this, it is something that anyone entering into a relationship with a Cuban should be well aware of.

The Dances of The Ancestors

Bodies glistening with sweat
Melodic rhythms, harmonious voices raised
Hands on skin as even the drums start to sing their own songs. Metal
on metal in driving syncopations to keep the rhythm together I am
transported between the worlds
The ancestors are here amongst us
I can hear them echoing from the ethers
I can see them moving through the bones and bodies in front of me
I can hear them crying and rejoicing in reunion here tonight

I am honored to feel embraced in their remembrance

The night air is cool and inviting. Cuba's winter is rarely colder than this and many Cubans are wearing jackets and scarves to shield themselves against the chilled wind that seems to blow every night in November. The air is abuzz with anticipation and community spirit. We are all anxiously awaiting the first drum to capture our attention and command our bodies into the rhythm's invocation. In front of me a stark concrete stage with a white concrete wall behind it is lined with a single row of chairs, and a few microphone stands and nothing more. The courtyard we are in is the back of the Casa de Cultura in Trinidad off of Calle Rosario. Surrounded on all four sides by white concrete walls, it makes for a perfect bouncy amphitheatre. There is no roof, and nothing frivolous or fancy about this space. Not one piece of decor, not one plant, nothing but a concrete floor, a concrete stage and concrete walls. During daytime hours, members of the Afro Cuban ballet and other artists use this space to rehearse for their performances for tourists. It is here, under the hot sun, tirelessly moving across the stage from one end to the other under the scrutiny of the director of the Ballet, that they perfect their shows. The gallons of sweat that have fallen onto this concrete are uncountable.

Jorge's little dreads bop by. He stops to embrace me heartily and thanks me for coming before disappearing into the tiny room that serves as backstage. It is also where I take my drum classes with Alexi and Alejandro. Looking around it appears I am the only tourist here. I feel honored and excited to be here as Trinifolk ramps up for its first night.

The Trinifolk festival happens every year in Trinidad, Cuba as a celebration of Cuban's diverse Afro-Caribbean-Spanish influenced roots. The celebration is dedicated to Amador Ramírez, founder of the Folkloric Ballet of Trinidad, and to Las Cuevas Orchestra, an emblematic musical group of the territory. This multidisciplinary festivity offers local residents an opportunity to enjoy the performance of some of the best and most devoted musical artists and performers from the Cuban provinces of Guantánamo, Las Tunas, Villa Clara, Santiago de Cuba, and Ciego de Ávila.

Performers and artists come from all over Cuba to share their knowledge, showcase their talents and be together as artists and cultural enthusiasts. In a week at Trinifolk, you can see a wide variety of cultural forms of music and dance from Santiago de Cuba, Camagüey, Cienfuegos, Havana, Pinar del Rio, and all the rural *(campesino)* areas as well. It is one of the highlights of the year culturally in Trinidad, and while poorly attended by tourists, it is highly attended by Cubans as a celebration of their cultural heritage. Casa de Cultura is located on Calle Rosario and for years has hosted this celebration of culture as well as many other regular community events including danzón, salsa classes, art classes and more.

Finally, the lights dim and one spotlight sweeps the stage to get our attention. The light is a big old-school canister light, operated by a man standing in the center with a cigar hanging out of his toothless mouth. The night transforms into a stream of color, song, theatre, rhythm and dance that touches the very fiber of my soul. Colonial white flowing dresses, colorful garbs of the Orishas, swishing rainbow skirts, machetes, coconuts, fire, and rum being spit across the audience all mesmerize and captivate the audience. This is Cubans celebrating their heritage, honoring their ancestors who dance through their bones, and sing through their voices, lifted together in ecstatic fervor uniting hearts and minds as one people.

There are performers on stage, but there is no separation of audience and performer in the hearts of those present. More than once, an audience member comes onto the stage to kiss the feet or tap the forehead of a dancer in acknowledgement of respect and familial love. Theirs is a bond that goes beyond anything I can relate to, yet I feel part of it in the depths of my being. My teachers are amongst the drummers, Alexi and Alejandro perform with several of the groups, and Jorge dances with his troupe from Ciego de Ávila as well as some of the other groups. I am in the company of true masters, and they are portals into worlds beyond this world in what they hold inside.

Seeing Jorge and the others dance was a portal to another world. Every inch of his body quivered and shook in perfection with the rhythm as he danced Guaguancó, yambu, and other folkloric forms

I had never seen. By far he was one of the most animated of all the dancers there. His big eyes would open wide and his nostrils would flare. He was the perfect embodiment of his culture's stories. Their dancing took me back in time. In their movements, I saw the Africans in their blood. Visions flowed through my mind watching and listening to the drums. It was as if I was witnessing the very history of this island through the dances and songs. I could feel the connection directly from the Motherland. I could see the slaves dancing and sweating in the fields. I could see the very evolution of the culture, through the many revolutions Cuba has endured, as they fought with machetes and sticks for their freedom. I could feel the suffering and challenges they went through in every movement they made. I was moved to tears more than once.

After the show Jorge and I shared the rest of the evening together. We laughed and danced all night. We walked and talked a lot. In spite of my pathetic Spanish, we were able to connect on deep topics. We talked about relationships, integrity, trust, and how important good communication is. I discovered a kindred spirit in this short, stocky man with long dreads and big happy eyes. He is a drummer and dancer, and part of the National Ballet of Ciego de Ávila. He invited me to visit him there. I accepted wholeheartedly.

Late in the night, he walked me home with his arm around my waist. He felt like a really good friend and a creative ally through the love we share of music and dance. It was a sense of relief for me that we both knew that I could not invite him in.

It is illegal for a Cuban national to enter a tourist's room without being officially registered as a guest.[12] It is not encouraged that they should consider registering or entering unless there is an established relationship. Both the owner of the Casa, and Jorge would be at risk. The government has very strict policies around Cuban interactions

---

12   2012 This was true in 2012. It was highly scrutinized and watched for Cubans to enter tourist residences. Now, some laws were changed and restrictions loosened, if a Cuban National is registered in the book each house is required to submit a report on it's guests, with their ID number documented, can enter with tourists if they are partners or spouses or family.

with tourists. Love has nothing to do with it. This is strictly controlled under the premise of protecting the tourists against Cubans who might have mal-intentions or who might be looking to find a way to get themselves off the island.

Cubans can be arrested and taken to jail for spending the night with a foreigner. The owner of the house can be fined up to $1,500 for one infraction. The owner of the casa runs the risk of losing their license to rent to tourists as well. There are eyes everywhere in Cuba, so most Cubans who associate with tourists do not take the chance of getting caught. It is well-known that there are many Cubans within the community that work undercover for the police, providing information for payoffs and special favors. Even in the dark deep part of night when you think everyone else is asleep, someone may in fact be watching. Someone knows exactly what is going on, and if that someone wants to make trouble, they know exactly how to do it.

And so, our night ends here, arm in arm, a new friendship formed. For me, it's perfect. I am silently grateful right now for the law being what it is. He kissed me goodnight and left me at my door feeling full, exhausted and totally content. In a few days, he will return to Ciego de Ávila. I am excited to go there and see his world one day soon.

I went to bed with a huge smile on my face again, warmed all the way through my being.

Beloved Brother

His perfectly sculpted body lays in front of me, sprawled out and shirtless. His widened eyes watch my fingers type as his fingers twiddle with his dreadlocks. I look up occasionally from my work just to drink in the sight of his perfect form. It is hard to focus on my work. He is beautiful in every way. He is strong, contemplative, deep and sensitive, and just the right amount of protective about me without being controlling or jealous. He is attentive, present, kind, appreciative, funny, sensitive, and physically perfect from head to toe. We drum together, dance together, laugh together and have a friendship that needs no special reason to be.

Jorge is a professional musician and dancer. Everything with him is natural, comfortable and effortless, healthy and pure. His eyes devour my heart and leave me quiet and content. We have an easy, fun connection that is drama free and tender. He is someone I can just enjoy relaxing and dancing with and know there will never be any drama because our connection is not one that will light that kind of fire in either of us. His affectionate playful way is refreshing, healing and just pure fun. He offers me a stark contrast to Fernando's heavy serious drama, and I love it.

Cubans are loving and familial by nature. It is not only common, but it is considered normal here for men and women to have multiple relationships with different dynamics to fit different needs. A woman may have several novios or amigos, but only one husband, and vice versa. Each relationship fulfills a unique need and while it is not often openly discussed, and usually kept discrete, it is very often quietly accepted (and even expected) from both men and women alike.

Christina, her mother, and I have talked for hours and hours about this topic over countless cups of coffee.

In regard to physical or sexual relationships, there is an unspoken acceptance of polygamy and polyamory here that reaches back to the African roots of the culture. Stepping outside of my own Catholic up-bringing, the truth is that it makes sense to me. I have often wondered why we expect one person to give us everything we need. How much stress does it put on our relationships when we expect one person to meet all of our complex multifaceted needs in intimate relationships? How liberating would it be if we were able to love freely in a more divine way and to allow each relationship to bring us what it is meant to bring without expecting it to be the one and only?

I have never really resonated with this idea of only loving one person forever. When I think of love, I think of the Divine. You can call it God or Jehovah, or whatever you want, but to me love is divinity and the source of all creation. Love is so powerful that it allows everything else to exist because in love there is no fear. Love is not afraid of losing anyone, it is not insecure or jealous. It fears nothing, because love knows that nothing is greater than itself. No force can create life, heal and bring light into the darkness the way that love can. Love, or "God" if you must, loves without discernment. God does not pick one, it loves all unconditionally.

So if we are to be, or act *in the likeness of God,* then practicing a higher love is part of the game. Attachment is not love. As humans, we too often confuse and collapse these two into each other. In these past few years of being single, I have been exploring relationships and different ways to share intimacy and love outside of physical/sexual connections. I have discovered that it is absolutely possible to love multiple people sincerely, deeply and passionately, and each in unique ways. I have discovered that different archetypes of men serve me in different ways and that to expect one man to fill all my needs only sets me up for disappointment.

Coming from a culture that very much equates love with sex in romantic relationships, I have also become passionate about finding ways to share love that are not sexual. The dance has become my sanctuary in this exploration. The intimacy and passion we can share through dancing is often more intimate than sex, which is not always a pure expression of intimacy at all.

I have learned that I do not need to be physical or sexual with a man to be able to enjoy loving him. Often it seems human beings have a tendency to completely bypass the deeper purpose of a relationship by jumping into sex without understanding the nature of what the relationship is truly meant to be.

In Cuba, it is the norm for men and women to have more than one lover, and more than one significant person in their lives. Many, if not most, Cubans, married or not, have auxiliary relationships outside of their primary relationships that last for years and often entire lifetimes. It is understood, and expected, and while few of them will openly discuss or admit this, it is something that anyone entering into a relationship with a Cuban should be well aware of.

There are also layers of secrecy, I call it a "hush code", that protect these relationships for the stability of communities and families. I am not advocating for it, nor am I in any way saying it is right. It is a personal decision for each person on how they live their lives. Throughout history, these types of extended relationships have been the foundation of African villages and tribal cultures around the world. Polyamory has deep roots that are still bearing fruit here in Cuba. In African communities it actually worked for the preservation and sustenance of the tribe or villages and here in Cuba, it serves that same purpose in its own unique way.

The irony is that while there is a quiet acceptance of this that is unspoken, jealousy is extreme and often very publicly displayed. It is far too common for a partner to expect the very devotion that they do not give to their own partner. Often the more jealous a person is, the more that person is likely to be entertaining (mentally or physically) other relationships outside of their primary one. While many call this "machismo" when related to male jealousy and possessive behavior, I need to make it very clear that in Cuba at least, it is not just the men who are jealous, possessive and fooling around on their primary partner behind closed doors. It is important to realize that the women play this game just as much as the men in Cuba. They can also be just as jealous, controlling and possessive as the men, and often more vindictive and sneaky.

In Cuba, relationships are everything. The very fabric of the community is woven out of a complex system of relationships. Cubans cherish and value their loved ones above all else. While it is common for people to have multiple intimate relationships at one time, Cubans very much also value devotion and loyalty in their relationships. There are, of course, also marriages and partnerships that are models of fidelity, trust and integrity through the course of their time together. In essence, it's the same everywhere with human relationships. The primary distinction for me is that in Cuba people have little else to focus on, and little exposure to the greater issues of the world outside of their direct contact, so relationships can become dramatic and consuming very quickly.

Glimpses In: A Visit to Ciego Ávila

"*Toca, toca,*" *he* says to me, pointing to the bucket of water in the shower stall. I touch it.

"Gracias," I manage to say with sincerity in spite of my irritation that the water is just barely warm. I am cold, and I want a hot shower more than anything else right now.

"Beautiful, yes?" he says with a heart filled with sweetness.

I know he is proud to offer this simple thing to me, so I hold back the spoiled demanding bitch in me, and say, "Si, gracias, esta perfecta amor."

I am both humbled and irritated being here. I left Trinidad to visit Jorge in his world in Ciego de Ávila to see a little more of Cuba from the inside out. Here, in his family's humble home, I am experiencing a returning to the roots of basic humanity that is poignant, if not a little painful. In spite of my frustrations, this experience is such a good reminder of how incredibly spoiled I have become by modern culture's luxuries and conveniences. It makes me acutely aware of how many little things I take for granted almost every day at home: simple things like a hot shower, toilet paper, or fresh, clean air that is not heavy with the smell of decay.

The shower is a stall only. None of the fixtures in the entire house produce water. Dangling above my head, there is a bare pipe with a pair of pink panties hanging from it where once perhaps there was a shower head. True to Cuban standards, the toilet has no seat. Since coming to Cuba, I have been getting pretty good at peeing standing up. It is not dirty really, just old and more primitive than I am accustomed to. This kind of bathroom is far from uncommon in Cuba however. Most Cubans live in conditions like this and quite often worse.[13] The casa particulars and hotels that tourists stay in are a huge step up from how the majority of Cubans live in Cuba, especially when you get outside of the tourist zones where real Cuban life is happening.

I spent a good part of the evening trying to avoid hanging out where the family was only because the smell of animal feces and urine is the strongest there. Where they like to sit to chat is directly in front of the pig pen. The odor is overpowering and it flows through the house from the open windows that face the pig pen. It almost knocks me out every time I walk through the house. Finally, I have to surrender or I feel like I am being too rude. To avoid the foul smell, I consciously breathe mostly through my mouth all night. I would never want to offend them or their openhearted generosity in any way.

This is one of the things that I do not really understand in Cuba that I have experienced multiple times. Families often seem to hang out in the stinkiest part of their yards where the animals eat and defecate, and where piles of rotting food are strewn about. They are apparently oblivious or accustomed to the intensity of the odorous air they are sucking in. Always, right around the corner, 10 feet away there is a clean, clear space, or a vacant porch where the air is fresh, the ground is clean and the space is far more inviting on every level. I do not understand it, but I have noticed it in many places and homes I have visited in Cuba. Perhaps it is part of the spirit of inclusiveness

---

13 The cost of fixing a bathroom in Cuba can be prohibitive for most Cuban families to afford. In 2019 I worked on a project for a bathroom remodel, and the cost of a basic fix up was over $3000. Many Cuban families will never see that much money in their entire lives. Finding materials to do the work can be the most difficult part. We had to drive to three provinces, and bring things in from the USA to complete this project.

that permeates the culture, and the animals are not excluded from that. I recall also experiencing this in India where the animals often lived inside the homes, and also in parts of Latin America.

The whole family was present to meet me, and both of his brothers had to dance with me to be sure that I could actually dance. It turned into a Cuban family night of *meet the foreigner*, with everyone showing off, dancing like crazy as bottles of rum flowed generously. I was having so much fun, that I quickly forgot all about the strong smells of the animals and fully enjoyed myself. We danced deep into the night until everyone was exhausted as plates of food were passed around during breaks. A family night *en casa*, Cuban style, is a special treat always.

Jorge's mother sits at the table in their small humble kitchen. Her head collapsed into her hand. She is sitting in front of the TV, but she is sleeping. Her thin face shows the weariness of poverty. Dressed in a dingy cotton nightgown that she has worn all day, cooking and cleaning, with a cloth tied around her hair and her mouth hanging open slightly, she touches my heart in a poignant way.

I imagine for a minute living the life she has lived here in this house, raising her children. I imagine how it has been, year upon year, dealing with men who drink every night to get drunk. Men with loud voices and boisterous heckling all expecting her to feed and serve them upon demand. I realize I cannot even begin to relate to her life. A part of me wants to take her in my arms, just to comfort her.

Her husband, Jorge's father, died several years ago of cancer, leaving her alone. I do not know if Jorge stays with her to help her and keep her company or because he has no other options, but likely it is both. I see that there is much he could do in his free time, which he has plenty of, to help her and fix up the house more. I know that money is always the excuse, and often also the reality. I see boxes of tile and concrete laying around, so obviously there is some intention brewing to fix things up. While it is easy to assume that the materials are already here and it is just the labor that's needed, in Cuba it could be that the one or two things needed to actually start the project might be impossible to find.

"You should put your mother to bed soon." I tell Jorge, seeing his mother collapsing over herself dozing off in the chair. He gets up and wakes his mother to get her to bed. He is kind to her, and it is easy to see that his gentle demeanor is due to her love. She raised a good man, and I love her for that. He is kind, sweet, intelligent and easy to talk with. I know that men like him do not happen without the love and kindness of their mothers. His grandmother lives with them also. The brothers take turns giving her baths and taking care of her.

His brothers live close by, one next door and the other across the street. Both of them have nicer homes, more fixed up and cleaner. They have worked hard and saved money to escape something that Jorge still lives in. I cannot help but both admire and wonder about this. His roots are humble. He has some idea of what else is possible, yet he has accepted his reality and does not seem to see much of a distinction between one and the other.

After his mother is put to bed, he and I curl up together in his humble room under the fan at high speed and talk for a few hours before falling asleep. He is refreshing to me, comfortable, safe, and not trying to seduce me or coerce me into sex. He seems perfectly content to just cuddle and appreciate being close to me without needing anything more than the companionship. This is a rare man indeed. Slowly, he is winning my trust and love more and more in his ability to be a gentleman with me. His body feels so good next to mine. His soft snore lulls me into a deep sleep, feeling nurtured and adored in the arms of a man who has become a good friend and ally.

Ciego de Ávila is a picture perfect city. It is clean, and feels elegant, like a city on the rise. It is the capital of the province of Ciego de Ávila and lies on the Carretera Central highway, on a major railroad. Its port, Júcaro, lies fifteen miles south-southwest on the coast of the Gulf of Ana Maria in the Caribbean Sea. It was part of the Camagüey Province until 1976, when Fidel Castro's government made it the capital of the newly created Ciego de Ávila Province.

Central Ciego de Ávila is used for cattle ranching. Elsewhere in the province, sugar, pineapples and citrus fruit are grown. Pineapples are the staple crop, but sweet potatoes, potatoes, yucca, plantains, and bananas are also cultivated for national consumption[14]

Riding through the city this morning from Jorge's house in the bici-taxi, I am a little sad that I am leaving. I woke up feeling like my body had been beaten by a heavy board, with a splitting headache, heavy cramps and low back pain screaming at me. All I want is to get back to Trinidad, and be alone, and quiet in my casita.

Jorge accompanies me to the center where my transport options live for returning to Trinidad. He explained to me last night that the only truly economically priced option for a ride back is one of the Cuban people mover trucks. I am not living on a normal tourist budget in Cuba, and $70 for a taxi back is out of reach for me with the amount of time I still want to stay in Cuba. Honestly, even if I was on a tourist budget, I am more interested in experiencing how Cubans actually live and commute than I am in comfort and convenience.

The truck is a big commercial size truck, the kind that would be a dump truck or a construction truck used to haul materials in the US, but of course this is an old classic 1960s style. The back of the truck has been adapted to be a transport vehicle for people. There are long rough wooden planks running the length of the back and handles above on a metal frame for standing passengers to hold on to when the seats are full. It is topped with canvas for some wind and weather protection, with some cutouts for windows, and a back door with a few steps that fold down for passengers to exit and enter.

"Nunca, para mi, no me gusta," (Never for me, I do not like it.). Jorge says. I get on the over packed truck and prepare myself for the adventure at hand.

"Are you sure this is a direct ride?" I ask him in my broken Spanish.

"Menos que una hora amor, seguro." (Less than an hour I am sure) He responds to me with total confidence. I have a sinking

---

14   Source: Wikipedia

feeling in my gut that the journey from Ciego de Ávila to Trinidad will take at least twice that long in this heavy, slow truck. I am torn between getting off and running for a taxi and paying the price or sitting through hours of painful jolting bumps on a metal seat with no cushions, packed in like a sardine with sixty others with menstrual cramps and a skull-splitting rum induced hangover headache.

The truck takes off. I feel like death. The cramps in my low back and belly are screaming at me. It is hot and uncomfortable. The truck is packed full of people. Someone close to me smells like horse manure. I close my eyes to meditate, and I commit myself to changing my attitude on the ride. I let the miles slowly melt away my pain and anxiety and eventually relax in spite of the pain my body feels.

Two hours later, exactly twice as long as the trip is on a normal direct bus, I arrive in Sancti Spiritús for my transfer to a taxi to Trinidad. Arriving in Trinidad again felt like a homecoming. My whole body exhaled in relief to be back. The rolling mountains, the smell of the sea, the cobblestone streets and horse-drawn carriages, and the music were welcoming to my body, mind and soul all at once.

December 21, 2012: The day the world did not end...again

I am at peace. I am present to the comforting moments of silence just before dawn. I am awaiting the first call of "Hay, pan" and before long, I hear that familiar voice and call of the local bread vendor echoing down the cobblestone streets. Soon after the first dog barked, the wind came calling. The new house I moved to is lovely for being able to enjoy the sounds of the wind. I welcome her: my Oya breathing life and inspiration into me once again.

I feel clear, happy and content today in a new way. Perhaps my birthday, which has long been a prophesied day for 2012 supposedly marking a big energetic shift in the cosmos, truly marked the end of an epoch.

I wonder what all my friends back home are doing on this auspicious day. I can envision the same scenario I have experienced countless times in Boulder. They are all talking spiritual stuff about the changes and the shifts in the world. Everyone is telling each other how incredible and amazing it all is. December 21, 2012 has finally arrived. They gather in a circle, hold hands and pray together waiting for some amazing moment of shift. They dance all night in celebration of the awaited day and moments and likely still woke up today in the same reality.

In Cuba, absolutely nothing happens. The world has not ended or even shifted for Cubans at all. They are still dealing with the same problems, the same dramas and the same lack of resources that they have been managing with for decades. They are listening to the same music, eating the same rice and beans, and living more or less the same day, over and over again. December 21, 2012 meant nothing to them here. They have never heard about it, so no one was too concerned about the end of the world on my birthday. Bottles of rum passed freely, the dancing was high energy nonstop, and December 21, 2012 was just like every other night.

In fact, nothing has changed much here for many years. If the rest of the world ended it might be days or weeks before I would even hear about it, so all I can do is trust the feeling of peace and contentment in my heart that all is well in the world. I cannot deny it is part of what I love about living here. There is nothing but what is here and now. This forced disconnection from the rest of the world serves me well. The insane neurosis that has become normal in the western world to know about every little thing that happens, every moment of every day, has never held much allure for me. I find it more distressing than comforting most days to hear about another bomb, another murder, another school shooting, or another disaster. Thanks to our overactive media and news channels, I now am more than aware that these horrors are happening all the time. To have to see the visuals, hear the audio, and have everyone around me constantly reacting and conversing about the seemingly unending string of atrocities happening in our world has never done much good for me.

Cell phones, incessant texting and email checking are time suckers. I can honestly say that I have not at all missed access to these in any way whatsoever. In fact, I could easily give them up for the rest of my life. It sounds absolutely dreamy and divine to return to the roots of natural living: walking to my friend's house when I want to talk and getting to greet people along the way. Visiting in person and sharing a meal rather than catching some tidbit about what someone had for lunch on Facebook is much more rewarding for me on every level. If I never got back online again, I would not be upset at all. I find that there is more peace available to me when I am just present to what is present in my world, in the present moment.

I am in love, deeply, with this way of life that Cuba has shown me. I love walking to visit my friends in their humble homes, sipping coffee or rum, and dancing in living rooms. I love walking to go out at night. I love that I can buy my fruits and vegetables fresh every day from the vendors that pass by my house for less than $3 a day. I love that I get to eat ripe delicious fruit and vegetables free of Monsanto's nasty hands. I love that all day and all night music rings through the streets from every house, every restaurant and from many of the bici-taxis. I love that I stroll past a home and peek in to see the woman of the house dancing in her living room with her broom or mop as she's cleaning up. I love that here the people value each other, take care of each other and care to ask how you are every day. I love that they sincerely listen when you respond. In short, I really just love the Cuban lifestyle.

I wonder if this love affair with this rock called Cuba can have any real potential. Reality forces me to consider the realities of my life: my debt, a community of people that are counting on me to return, friends who love me, my mother who would possibly have a heart attack at the thought of me marrying a giant Cuban man with flailing arms. My father would disown me. I am quite sure of it.

And yet, all I can think of is how to make this crazy Cuban dream come to life, even if just for a year or two. All I can think of is that it might actually be possible and that I would be more than happy to find a way to make it so. I am happier here. Life makes more sense to me here in many ways. The people relate to each other more like an extended family and although there are cultural differences, there is a resonance I feel here that is undeniable in my lifestyle preference.

I know that life here would have unique and intense challenges in a more permanent reality.

It is crazy. The whole thing is absolutely insane. Yet, I am always mentally entertaining the possibility. The dream is very alive.

Amor Part 2

One of his hands covers the whole small of my back, and the other is wrapped all the way around me holding me close, with profound tenderness. Being in his arms is pure intoxication. He looks like a god to me. Every inch of him is perfectly proportioned. His luscious full eyelashes, big full lips, and smile light up my world.

"Tell me, what do you need? I want to know. I want you to tell me what you need in a relationship so I can give you that, Ok? Maybe we leave together when we go. Maybe we live in Miami, maybe Colorado? Maybe Spain? What do you think? Maybe we come back to Cuba? I am serious. What do you think?" Fernando says to me, looking up at me.

I smile but say nothing. These last two weeks have been a bit more of a rollercoaster than I prefer with him. My confidence is pretty low that this relationship can last at this point. He continues, more seriously.

"You have a lot of amigos, I no like. I want to feel secure, and when we are out like you are with me. I want to feel seguro, and you too segura, you know segura?" He asks me, his eyes sincere and super soft.

"Si, si amor, entiendo." I do know: it means secure, for sure, certain, together. It touches my heart. The idea of it is beautiful, endearing and even romantic.

Sadly, the reality of what I have experienced with him in these past few weeks is another thing entirely. He has been beyond difficult, riding the edge of impossible for me. He has managed to push every button imaginable in me, from triggering my insecurities with all his women friends, to random, drunken disappearances, to breaking my trust in his integrity by not showing up when he said he would or acting in ways that are not acceptable for me.

It is hard to know what aspects of the impossibility are cultural and what aspects are personality-driven in moments. The chemistry between us is electric and tangible. If it was channeled for a creative project or something positive it would be unstoppable. Chemistry alone does not make for a healthy relationship, however. He is often angry and almost always, when he is drunk, he finds a reason to be angry. Since he seems to be drunk almost every day, almost every day with him has been a challenge of dealing with his crazy making. As much as I am in love with him, more so, I'm kind of grossed out by it all.

My response to his insanity has been withdrawal and distance. After all, I came to Cuba to study the culture, language and music, not to get involved in crazy making or drama with Cuban men. However, it is beginning to feel like they are inseparable and all part of my education here. Everything in Cuba is based on relationships. Love and attraction are constantly in the ethers here, and while many will argue with me, Cubans love deeply, bordering on obsessively.

I have to wonder if part of this is because there is so little other stimulation or access to the greater world and community. Their world, especially in the smaller villages and pueblos, is very small. All that matters to them is their relationships because they often do not have much else at all to do or focus on. Many of the women rarely leave the house except to go for food or things they need. The men are accustomed to their women being available at all times for them. The men are more free in the streets and come and go as they please and are not expected to be as available as the women.

The musicians and artists I know are a little more open in the way they love, and it seems to me that they are less obsessive and controlling in their relationships. Perhaps it is because they have a focus outside of their relationships that requires their devotion and time. Many Cubans do not work because there is no work for them or because they would rather not work than work for practically nothing anyway. Considering that the average wage for full time employment sits between US $15-25 a month, it is understandable.

Often they may have a small business selling things out of their homes, but again this keeps them mostly home and in a very small container of relating. Very few Cubans have the resources to travel or even take day trips to the beach or mountains. For many Cubans, life offers little inspiration. Day in and day out, for years on end, it is like the same day over and over for them. Creating and sustaining some drama in their relationships can often be the only real adventure they can have in their lives. When one can see through that lens, the drama that is so common in Cuban relationships is somewhat understandable. I am convinced that often, it is the only thing they can find to save them from the mental agony of total boredom with life. They can obsess on things that we in the modern world simply would not have the time to even think about. The slightest word or gesture here can be cause to create a world of drama that can quickly become explosive and last a lifetime. For all their tough exterior and loud talk, Cubans are very sensitive people. While they can be extremely accepting and forgiving, it is also true they can hold grudges for a lifetime over very trivial things.

The insights I have gained through the relationships I have had in Cuba are ones that could be gained no other way. By nature, I am a lover and a lover of all things relational. I study psychology constantly, within myself and in everyone around me. I am a constant student, watching, learning and hopefully improving myself along the way.

With Fernando, it is another layer of confusion as he lives in Spain and has some experience with modern culture; yet his heart and mind are firmly rooted in Cuban culture. I can see that my behavior when applied within his cultural context would be very confusing, just as his behavior applied with my cultural lens has been quite confusing. I have been out almost every night dancing with countless men in front of all his friends and community. Then I disappeared and left Trinidad for almost a week to get away from him, thinking he would be back in Spain before I returned. Much to my surprise, and frustration, he was the first person I ran into when I returned.

I have been very much playing hard to get with a man who is accustomed to having women fall at his feet, always be available and do whatever he wants them to do. I have distanced, isolated, withdrawn and rebelled against him in every way imaginable. At the same time, I know he can feel that I am passionately in love with him.

So who has been more impossible? I think we both met our match in some way.

His hand on my thigh is comforting. I kiss him softly on the lips, and he smiles an enormous smile lighting up his entire face.

"I am very happy," he says.

"Me too, amor." He lifts me straight up, five feet in the air, and kisses me deeply, total caveman style with a smile that melts me. I breathe him in like the air I have needed for weeks and then reluctantly let him go.

Today I understand something of him on a different level and I am in admiration of it, in spite of my desire. He is thinking much longer term than I am. Clearly, sex is not a priority for him. He feels like we have the rest of our lives to explore that world. In regard to sex, he can take it or leave it which is just totally foreign for me in a man, especially one with such sexual power and draw. How could it be that with all the crazy sex-driven men in Cuba, I met two who are actually balanced and healthy around their approach to sex? I feel pretty grateful for that.

"Sex is nothing," he said to me one time, "I can have sex anytime. I want to have a serious relationship with you."

It is such a different paradigm for me. I have gotten overly accustomed to sex being a foundational pillar of my relationships. This dynamic with Fernando is making me take a good hard look at myself, my culture and what I have accepted as *normal* from men for so many years.

In spite of the impossibility of this relationship working, I am absolutely head over heels in love with this dramatic giant. I feel myself dreaming up all kinds of possibilities of how he and I can create something amazing here. There is so much potential and because he already has his citizenship outside, I know he is not looking to me to get him out of Cuba, which is a big relief. Yet in my rational mind, the wise woman in me asks, "How many heartbreaks have I endured for men with *potential?*"

Women are the masters at seeing men for their potential and being blind to the reality of what they truly are. (Perhaps men do this too, I cannot speak to that as a woman.) We fall in love with an ideal man, one that is often more of a figment of our imaginations than anything else. We fall in love with a story that we make up to glorify our choice of a partner or validate our attraction to the bad boys. We go out of our way to put him on a pedestal of being everything we ever wanted, or of being able to become that perfect prince charming with our loving care and support.

Sadly, it does not work. It cannot work. It is nothing more than a fantasy we create to trick ourselves into staying in relationships that will only leave us sad, disappointed, frustrated and hurt when the man turns out to be just exactly who he always really was in time. If there is true love, that kind I spoke of earlier, that sees behind the delusions and projections we like to plaster on others, then you can at least salvage a friendship from it all and maybe, if you're lucky, something more.

I have much to learn from the Cuban ways. While some might see it as more coldhearted, I see it as just being real with the reality. If we spent even half as much energy just accepting people and things as they are as, we do in trying to change them, we might just find one of the secrets to long-lasting peace and tranquility. I affirm to love without expectation and to focus on what is real and present with Fernando and let him demonstrate his potential. A wise man once told me, "When someone shows you who they are, believe them."

The reality is I am ready for a life-partner, and there is a strong desire within me to find a partner in Cuba that could open the door to the possibility of me living here one day, at least part time. I can not deny that. I want to live here more and have this as an option to return to forever. Truthfully, I do not want to live in my country anymore. The overstimulation, and the hollowness of the culture aches in me. The pace of life, the isolation of how we live there, the constant depression I battle there, the quest for more, better, faster, harder: all of it just sickens me to my core. I am apparently more old-school in my ways than even I realized.

Can the solution really be hooking up with some big crazy Cuban man? I doubt it, at least not with this one. I am not sure yet what it is, but somehow if it's meant to be, I can only trust that it will come to pass. Attaching to a dramatic, gorgeous Cuban man is not going to be my salvation, of that I am sure.

Christmas In Cuba: Just Another Day

The day starts with the first cry of "*Hay pan*" in the streets before the first rooster crows. The following hours are a soft crescendo of sounds that add to the orchestra of daily life in Trinidad. I enjoy taking the mornings slowly: a cup of hot tea, time to write and reflect, meditate, stretch and prepare for my day slowly with no need to rush is invaluable.

It is Christmas Day, but nothing feels different in Cuba. I have not seen any Christmas trees, except in Christina's home. There are no twinkling icicles or colorful lights hanging from roofs, nor any low hanging mistletoe in doorways. Traffic is normal, the stores are still bare shelved, and no one is at all stressed about it. There is no concept of Santa, and thankfully, no rushing around like mad to try to buy gifts or decorations. Children are not looking for a reindeer-led sled in the sky, and there is no expectation of gift giving or obligatory, boring, family feasts. I have not felt any difference at all in the streets or in the vibe of the people here. Christmas in Cuba is just another day. It has very little significance here. Some families will enjoy dinner together but it is a very casual sharing. Many Cubans will be in the streets or in their homes watching television tonight just as they would be any other night. In Cuba the bigger celebration and more important holiday is *Fin de Año*, December 31, New Year's Eve. On New Year's Eve everyone will be together with their families at home sharing food, dancing in living rooms, and drinking countless bottles of rum and eating freshly roasted pork.

I am grateful to have escaped the need to shop, buy gifts and go through all the nonsense and stress of what this once holy day has become in my country. I loved Christmas when it was about sharing food and being together as a family. I have never loved the frantic stress that seems to build in the streets and city centers at this time of year. This year, I gave myself the gift of enjoying complete tranquility in the days and weeks before Christmas. I found peace in going to sleep early on Christmas eve and waking up this morning to the quiet rhythms of the morning. I sank into stillness, celebrating the real meaning of Christmas which is to unite with the Christ self or the higher light within. On this ordinary day in Cuba, I will celebrate Christmas by giving thanks for all the blessings I have experienced in the past years.

I am not Yelling, I am Cuban

The screaming child must have gone on for an hour this morning. It woke me early and was the only sound I could hear for a long time. It is hard to imagine what could be so horrible as to create that kind of response in a child for such an extended period of time. It is harder still to imagine that a child can have that much endurance to scream at that volume for that long. To imagine that a parent can endure that for so long without doing something to bring it to a close is possibly the most difficult for me to understand.

I got up and went to my yoga mat for my morning practice. In the courtyard behind mine, I could hear the neighbors fighting. I wondered how anyone could hear anyone when everyone was talking at once. There were at least three or four voices at once all seemingly in heated exchanges. Repeated choruses of "Mira," "Mira," "Mira." I imagined all of them trying to calm down one woman who was hell bent on getting her message across in spite of their attempts at trying to get her to listen and see things differently. The fight went on for about 15 minutes, then suddenly voices returned to normal and a softness returned to the air. Fully expressed, the woman had gotten it all out. She was calm again.

This is part of what I love about Cuba. If you want to scream and throw a tantrum for an hour here, chances are no one is going to stop you or even bat an eye at you. One night, I witnessed a French tourist having an incredible episode of freaking out. He was waving his arms and screaming at the Cubans, trying to pick fights and obviously completely drunk. It was quite a show, amusing but also a very ugly display of the European white male arrogance I disdain so much. The comedy in it for me, and what I enjoyed more, was seeing the complete lack of response from the Cuban people. For all his wanting to get attention, they did not even look at him. No one mentioned it nor did anyone seem to have any issue or concern about it. I was secretly hoping someone would just knock the guy out, to be honest. He was so belligerent and obnoxious, yet the Cubans could not have cared less. It was like he did not even exist.

Here, amongst the community, you are free to express yourself fully in your humanity and emotions. You can be happy, or angry, laugh or scream at the top of your lungs and no one cares too much. The irony for me is that this is a country without freedom of speech as a human right in the political sense, yet there is such an incredible acceptance for the freedom of expression in the community, family and social environments.

Cuban people talk loud and strong. They have no problem being very vocal in their joys, or frustrations. Their emotions are on display at almost all times and they do not try to sugarcoat anything. It is just normal and acceptable for people to have strong emotional reactions and responses to life, for better or worse. Almost always, they are loud. They speak passionately and with fervor, even about things that are not very significant. I saw a great T-shirt one day that said, *"I am not yelling, I am Cuban."* Public displays of charged expression and emoting are normal, and fully accepted. Yelling, cursing and sharing intensely passionate emotional moments are part of life here. Heated moments are common. There's a tolerance for full self expression as a normal part of the human experience, including conflict and harsh exchanges.

"We never say 'I am sorry'," my friend Christina told me one day when we were talking about some of the distinctions between my culture and hers. "It is normal here. We do not need apologies from each other like you do. We think it is strange to expect people to always talk calmly." It is part of the heart of Cuba that I love.

In the USA, it often feels like people are trying so hard to tiptoe around their feelings and the feelings of others, that no one is being real. All this spiritual and political correctness, while beautiful in idealism, seems to have created an environment where everyone is even more afraid of just saying what they really feel for fear of saying it incorrectly or offending someone somehow.

Who decided for us that we should be protected so much from reality and normal emotions? Who came up with this idea that we should never have our feelings hurt or be confronted with conflict or have to listen and witness someone truly expressing their anger, hurt or frustration in life? Why are we so easily traumatized when someone raises their voice even slightly at us? The more time I am in Cuba, the more I realize how sensitive we are and to what lengths we will go to avoid conflicts. We have lost the art of discussion and the ability to respect different perspectives without judgment.

Here no one is going to be tiptoeing around the truth, or other people's sensitivities. People here have a backbone strengthened by years of real difficulties and struggles to survive. They are not going to be wasting time trying to sugarcoat or soften up the reality of their feelings or emotions. They certainly are not going to take it personally every time someone is heated or frustrated about something not going their way. Life is difficult sometimes. It is just the way it is. So what? Big deal. There are other things that are more pressing and important. Finding food and keeping a few pesos in their pockets is hard and stressful beyond what many of us in the USA will ever understand. Stress is real. People get angry and upset. Sometimes people scream at each other and children cry for hours on end. This is life. Deal with it. It will pass. Peace will return. Tranquilo.

What I notice about arguments and heated moments here is that after the fire has passed, there is a tenderness of acceptance and shared humanity that returns quickly. No one is crying or feeling bad about anything on either side. There is an acceptance and a general feeling of, "Ok, well that was that, I'll see you later, un beso." Rarely do you see someone retreating to a bedroom and pouting over it or holding resentments for hours or days. The conflict transformation here is inevitable because people have to live together. There is nowhere to run and hide. For most of them, there is no way out. There is no way to escape each other, or leave your family to move to another state or country. You have your moments, spit your fire, receive your fire, scream and wave your arms around, shed your tears if you must. Then you sit down together, and have some rum or coffee, let the moment pass and return to normal life.

Ceremonia

Her face appears swollen. Her cheeks puff out with her lips pursed tightly together as her whole body pushes the air through them with strong heavy breaths. Her body is glistening with sweat. Her eyes roll back into her head. The drums grow more intense meeting her trance with willing instigation. Behind her, a young woman dressed in a tight white T-shirt starts flailing and stumbling. She is gently pushed into the center to heighten her trance. The drummers increase the energy. A third woman enters the center. The rest of us stand behind and around the three women in the center. We silently support them energetically, with strong minds, spirits and bodies aware and ready for whatever might come.

The living room is hot. The sun is beaming in through the open doors. Everyone is sweating. The floor is soaking wet, covered with rum, water and sweat. The singing and dancing are relentless. I stand in the corner, grateful to have been invited in, and respectful of the space.

Knowing eyes meet mine from every corner of the room. I am invited into the center by the matron of the ceremony. She sees me in my own rhythmical realm, recognizes me as one who knows, and pulls me into the center. For the first time in a Santería ceremony, I close my eyes and fully let go. I know I am safe here. My teacher is playing. All the men who are drumming have become acquaintances from other ceremonies I have been invited to witness.

I let the rhythm take me and allow my body to meet the drums fully. The chanting and perfect interplay of rhythmical melody are healing for me. I am home here with this music, these people, this ceremony. I still do not fully understand a lot of it on a cerebral level, but in the heart all is understood. There is much to learn, yet somehow it is home for me.

The music stops and the puffy-cheeked woman starts rambling. *"Como le di…"* she says every few phrases. She takes the woman next to me and starts to speak to her in Congolese. Everyone seems to understand except me. I know it is not Spanish but I listen to see if I can understand anything. I pray the puffy-cheek woman does not pick me next and start a discourse in this language with me. This goes on for a long time. I slowly back away from the center and find my way to sit outside to get some air and watch from a distance.

The drummers leave the room and come outside and sit on the step next to me to have a smoke. *"Como le di,"* the woman inside is still repeating. The people inside are listening. A man comes by and hands me a cup of something hot, in a thin plastic cup that should be melting but somehow is not. I sip it, and am delighted by the delicious flavor. A warming ginger chicken soup to nourish us after hours of intense dancing and trance.

Next a bag of candy is passed around. Everyone gets three candies. I don't really want them, but I take them and say thank you anyway. A few handfuls of candy are tossed into the street. After some time, the music starts again and the puffy-cheek woman, who I assume is a priestess of Santería, commences more of the ceremony. I have already been blessed and purified by a candle and fire. She comes around to all of us with more water from the bowl by the door filled with rose petals and washes us all clean. All the time she is dancing and keeping her feet in perfect time to the cacophonous swell of rhythm that is relentlessly pounding through all of us. All the time she is breathing heavily with big pouty puffy cheeks and tightly pursed lips combined with a look of consternation and frustration, almost bordering on anger. She is so dramatic and somehow adorable. I know it is all part of the trance. No one would dare laugh or even smile at her, not with that face. She is fully embodying her role.

The drums take us into new heights when my teacher sits down to play. He brings bold intense energy with huge arm-flailing hits and intent to push the level. He is watching us all as we move, working the energy with deliberation and a huge smile on his face all the while.

The priestess woman comes now with a big bowl of green foliage on her head. She spits rum all around us onto the floor. She takes the bowl off her head and spits on the foliage then thrashes the floor with it, and puts some outside the door. She is cleansing and purifying this room, and all in it. She thrashes some of the people, seeming carefully selected, with the foliage, throws some on the ground and dances more.

She comes next with a cigar and rubs us all down with it. She rubs my arms and legs with tobacco. I meet her eyes fearlessly, acknowledging our sisterhood in the rhythm. She pouts and nods at me. I am accepted here. I know my dancing and my spirit have shown them who I am.

Everyone is handed a large handful of rice from a huge bowl. The women put it in their bras, and the men in their pockets. I put mine in my pocket. Drool is spewing from her lips as she passes a coconut shell filled with rum. I do not really want to drink, but I do it anyway after dipping one finger in and dousing my forehead and back of my neck.

We continue to dance and sing together for hours, all of us finding our own healing together through music. I leave feeling lighter than I have in weeks with a huge smile in my heart and prayers ringing through my body in the afterglow.

The Infectious Sting of Cuba

It is an infectious sting.
First there's the bite. It comes quick and unexpectedly.
Then the itch starts and soon comes the long slow burn.
All you can think about is finding relief.

You treat it with time and money, attention and love,
music and rum, but somehow it spreads into your whole being.

It seems to increase in severity.
It deepens its impact on your whole life.
Everything starts to seem less important in comparison
to the infection running through your veins.
All thoughts and actions start to revolve around finding some relief
from the pain. It can leave a deep scar on your life,
and if you're lucky, it is a scar that has softened you.

It is a scar that seeks always to find you and remind you
of the things that matter the most in life.

This is the infectious sting of Cuba.

I spent the evening last night talking with a new friend, Linda, who has married a Cuban man and is living in Cuba. She is a lovely woman, intelligent and savvy. I could not help but wonder if she was some future reflection of myself.

"You're always the stranger here, you know. They accept you, but my husband's daughter, she still refers to me as 'the stranger.' I expect it will always be that way." Her face shows a resilient acceptance wrapped in disappointment.

"Nothing here is really as it seems. It's like anywhere, you know. People have layers. You think you know someone and then there's another layer. You never really know if they are your friend or if they are just seeing you as dollar signs. No matter what, you will always be the one expected to pay more for everything."

The music is so loud we have to practically shout at each other to talk. Casa de Música is filling up to a tight sardine can vibration. I am literally shoved into the table by the people behind me. I scoot my chair back claiming a little space for myself. There are many new faces, and unlike most nights here, it feels less like community and more touristy tonight. I know it is because we are reaching *Fin De Año* and there are a lot of tourists and Cubans returning home, all coming to Trinidad to celebrate.

"I came here first ten years ago," Linda says, her thick English accent and slow relaxed speaking is a pleasurable shift to my ears from the hard, fast Cuban Spanish.

"For four years I came every year. Then for a few years I took a break and did other things, but it never left my heart, you know. Two years ago, I came back with a friend, and I met my husband. Last year we got married. Sometimes it is hard. I do not always understand everything, and it will probably always be like that. I guess it is always going to be hard living in another country with a culture and a language that is not your own."

We share about the overabundance of drama in relationships here. Most of the people here have very little else to think about or focus on outside of their relationships. Life can get boring sometimes, and the drama keeps them entertained and occupied in a world where it seems nothing ever changes.

We talk about the freedom of sexuality and how it is the norm for most Cubans to have multiple partners. We talk about the black market and the strong police presence that, while making it very safe for us, also is beginning to rob us of the experiences we came here for. Dancing and enjoying the Cuban people socially is heavily moderated by the police presence and more and more Cuban people are not going out to dance or socialize as much, for fear of being arrested or harassed by the police.

We speak about the way that Cuba gets under your skin. Cuba is a place you either really get and love, or you really do not get and hate. Most people move through it so quickly they miss the real heart of the people and culture. It is only in slowing down and staying in one place that Cuba begins to unfold more fully to you.

I share with her that, for me, Cuba has been kind of an infectious addictive sting. She laughs, and I go on, indulging her in a little playful drama.

"First, there's the bite. It comes quick and unexpectedly. Once you've been bitten, it just courses through your system. You hurt, and ache. You find yourself always wanting just a little more of it; even knowing that it will very likely only bring more pain. You try to give it up and the withdrawal symptoms find you at all hours of the day and night. It is hard to focus on anything else. Everything starts to seem less important in comparison to the infection running through your veins." My friend is smiling as I share, nodding her head in acknowledgement to how this Cuba addiction happens.

"Then the itch starts and soon comes the long slow burn. All you can think about is finding relief. You treat it with another trip to try to "get over it." You give it more time, use more of your money to get back to it. You feed it with more attention and love, music and rum, but somehow it spreads into your whole being. It seems to increase in severity. It deepens its impact on your whole life."

"All thoughts and actions start to revolve around finding some relief from this constant driving pleasure and pain game. It can leave a deep scar on your life, and if you're lucky, it is a scar that has softened you. It is a scar that seeks always to find you and remind you of the things that matter the most in life."

"This is the infectious sting of Cuba."

Linda laughs wholeheartedly, "That's a perfect metaphor, it is really true you know." She says.

We speak about everything as sisters: reflections for each other of each other in many ways. She is living a life I am seriously contemplating trying to create. I am a reflection for her, of herself, a few years before she made the leap of faith. Unbeknownst to me at the time, she will become a lifelong friend and ally.

The Sanctimony of The Sacred

Her long brown hair flows down her back creating a stark contrast to the pale yellow dress she wears proudly. She is plump but not fat, her skin is soft brown, and perfectly smooth. She sits in a rocking chair next to me, her brown eyes framed in delicate, silver wire glasses. Her eyes are fixed on me for some time before she speaks.

"Do you speak English?" she asked me sweetly. "I can speak English with you, if you'd like. I am from here, but I live in Miami with my father now. My name is Gabriela." Her English was perfect. I was grateful to have someone to speak with before the ceremony started. Sometimes, it's a little awkward for me when I arrive at the home of someone I do not know to participate in a ceremony for their religion. There are so many questions I have yet to have answered about what is appropriate, what I should or should not do, what to bring as an offering, how to address people and what is expected of me. I am glad to get an opportunity to talk with Gabriela in English and ask her a few questions. Unfortunately, she barely gives me a chance to ask anything, she is so excited to talk. Her monologue informs me well, however, and I enjoy hearing her story.

"I love to travel. I want to see the world. I believe if you never leave your home and never see the world, you do not know anything. You have to understand the world more to be a better person. I want to go on a boat trip, where you study and go around the world." Gabriela says.

"Semester at Sea?" I ask her. "I know that program, it is incredible." I share with her a little of my experience doing similar programs when I was in college. I encourage her to follow through on it. Her father sits in the rocking chair next to her listening to us chat. I am touched by his presence and the way he empowers his child silently. I am not sure yet if he speaks English, but I imagine he does. Another young woman sits quietly next to me, listening attentively but saying nothing. I wonder if she, too, speaks English or if she is just curious enough to stay there listening.

"So you are interested in The Religion?" Gabriela asks me with sincerity.

"Yes," I say. "I am a drummer and also do a lot of ceremonies in my country with music and drumming. It's very different but similar in that we work with the elements and use music and drumming as the primary part of the ceremony. I am studying with Alejandro."

The mention of my teacher's name draws a smile to her face.

"Alejandro was at my ceremony for making the saint. I yelled at him and told him to play harder, because Elegua could not hear him." She smiled again. "I am the child of Elegua. You know in Santería we believe you have seven guardian angels that rule your head. You want to be good so that you do not have to come back again. Someone told me that this is my last life. I will not have to come back after this. I am glad that I am so young to be in Santería, this is a very good thing. I love religion, but I do not believe it is the only way to God. I believe that every religion is God. How can you say one person's God is better than another person's God? There are many different religions, and they are all God."

I am impressed with this young woman's wisdom and knowledge. Her confidence, presence and passion for religion and spirituality are akin to my heart and spirit. I know I have found a new friend in her.

"I am supposed to be in white, but I am not so old. I am seventeen, so I do not have to wear white all the time. Older people have done more bad things, made more bad decisions and need more purification. A seven year old, for example, has not made so many mistakes so he does not have to wear white all the time. I was very sick and The Religion made me well. I was very traumatized when my father left when I was seven. I would pass out and be unconscious for two or three days at a time. No one knew what was wrong with me, so my mother brought me to the Religion. I was baptized. You have to be baptized to be in Santería. I am a catholic also. Most Santos are catholic. It's part of our religion, you know. We use the saints as part of the Orishas."

I ask her about taking photos and if she can help me to know what is appropriate or not.

"You should never take a photo of anyone in white. They can not be photographed. The rest is OK." I am not convinced of that, and ask her to guide me whenever she feels I am inappropriate as I do not want to offend or step out of line.

"Excuse me," she says and leaves the room giving the young woman next to me an opportunity to chime in.

"Her English is very good." The young girl next to me says, "I speak English also, but not so good as her. She lives in a place she can practice every day. I live here."

"Your English is very good also," I say. She is a lovely young woman, with big bold eyes and a soft sensual energy to her. "And how long have you been practicing Santería?" I ask her.

"My mother brought me when I was a baby. I, too, was very sick. I cried all the time and had fits of anger that were harmful. My mother brought me to the religion and it healed me as well, so I believe in it. Now I am very calm." I was aware of her calm, present energy during my conversation with Gabriela, much like an enlightened presence sitting at my feet quietly listening and absorbing. We spoke for a few minutes before the ceremony started.

"Many people come to Santería for healing, yes?" I ask her.

"Yes, it is said that people are called to Santería when they need to be healed." I wonder what in me is needing healing, and why I am so called to this incredibly fascinating religion with cigars, rum and infectious rhythmical alchemy. There are many things that come to mind. My heart, my mind, my body and my cultural affliction from the USA possibly being the top of the list.

I hear the drums start outside. I excuse myself and get up to go outside to see what's going on. The drummers are all in a tiny eight by ten cement block storage shed with no light. I peek over the shoulder of Yovani, one of the musicians who is playing bell in the doorway. I see my teacher, Alejandro, glistening with sweat, already playing with maddening intensity, his arms flailing high into the sky before they hit the drum.

He brings such tremendous power and a fierce, yet joyous presence. Clearly, that is why he is so sought after for ceremony and keeps himself so busy working. He told me he has enough work now with ceremonies that he does not need to do any other work for money. He does ceremonies almost every day, and he is well-known throughout the region for his knowledge, wisdom and the special energy that he brings to the work.

The room is so dark I can not see anything but glistening skin. I finally make out an altar covered with chicken feathers and some green foliage in the corner of the room. They are blessing the offering. I am guessing that earlier chickens were sacrificed for the soup that will be offered later. After about twenty minutes, the drummers re-enter the courtyard and set up in the corner in the back, close to the pig pens that house three enormous hogs. The ceremony continues.

I notice all the men are together in the front, close to the drummers. The women are all tucked back behind them. The men are all dancing together in a circle, furiously pounding the cement with bare feet; most of them are shirtless. They are waving their arms and making eye contact with each other. Sometimes they seem almost confrontational, yet it is somehow jovial and understood between them that they are being men together.

My teacher Alejandro, and the biggest man there, who towers close to seven feet tall with a girth as big as a truck tire, bellows cantos (songs) at each other with waving arms. I am impressed with my teacher's power to quiet this man who towers a good two feet over him when he tries to change the song. Alejandro is clearly the master of the music here. He shuts the big man down more than once with a wave of his arm and a strong "No."

This is different from any other ceremony I have been to. I can feel the masculine presence being invoked, but I do not know much really about what is going on or the intention of this particular ceremony, only that it feels different and more male-dominated. Gabriela told me earlier that it would be "scary" and that it was a ceremony to bring in the New Year since tomorrow will be Dec 31. That's about all I know. Most of the other ceremonies I have attended are more balanced with the men and women dancing side by side and a much stronger feminine presence in the dance. Here, the rum is being passed constantly, cigars are torched up, nostrils are flaring and the energy is intense and most definitely masculine and warrior-like.

The giant and another large man draw Yoruba symbols on the ground with chalk. Everyone gathers around in a circle to watch, singing and dancing all the while. Rum is spat into the sky and is raining down on us. The cigar smoke creates billowing pillows of smoke floating off into the sky. The song changes and everyone dances furiously on top of the symbols, until they disappear as dust in the wind and the intention of the symbols is pounded into the earth.

Suddenly a large man falls to the ground. The music intensifies and everyone gathers around him, watching. His body moves in a way that is not human. He moves more like a snake. He is lying face down on the cement. I am amazed that a man so large can slither so well. It is almost as if he is on wet glass sliding slowly across a smooth surface as if on wheels or skates. In reality, he's on concrete, it is rough and he is a huge man. I know he has gone into possession.

He slithers into the concrete shed where the chicken feathered altar lives. A few moments later, he re-emerges dressed in a red loin cloth and a red bandana. He has a cigar in his mouth and the same big pouty lips, drooling mouth and puffy breath I have seen in other ceremonies with the possessed. I want to film all of this, but I do not dare pull out my camera now. I would not even think of it, but I can't help but wish that I had some secret agent on the rooftop to film this incredible ritual.

The towering seven-foot giant lights two purple candles and mounts them inside the bandana on top of the other man's head.

Throughout the ceremony, he relights them many times and appears to be the assistant to the possessed. An incredible ceremony ensues, the likes of which I have yet to see anywhere. First, everyone is blessed by water and rum. In turn, they fall to the ground, belly down, at this man's feet, then they get up and bump shoulders with him. He turns them around once, then grabs one wrist in each of his hands and flaps their arms hard. He then bumps their heads hard with his and sends them back into the circle.

Then everyone is purified, flapped and swished with big leafy green branches. The women all hold their breasts as they are being cleansed. Then comes the discourse and the magic. The music stops and the man starts to talk in some language that is not Spanish, but I believe to be Congolese. Everyone responds in a chorus of acknowledgement and the music begins again.

Another purification ceremony begins, this time with a coconut. Everyone is rubbed down and we are singing *Coco limpia*. Alejandro hands me a shekere. Once the instrument is in my hands, I feel like I am home here, bringing my own energy to the ceremony in the way that is the most natural for me.

Again the music stops. The man starts talking again. He picks up a white dinner plate, rubs it on the giant's bald forehead, and passes it around for us all to breathe on. I add my breath to it and my musician friends giggle with me, knowing I have no idea what I am doing, but doing it anyway because it is the thing to do. I think probably they have no real idea either why everyone is breathing on a plate. It seems that we all realize this is a show and that the possessed man can ask us to do just about anything, and most everyone here will do it. We share some knowing smiles but try to appear serious.

Alejandro passes me a smile and pats me on the shoulder lovingly. The giant man is now filling a glass with ash, coffee grounds and some kind of fizzy bubbly liquid which I imagine is tonic water. He holds the glass up so everyone can watch the bubbling. I think of alchemy and the elemental aspects of nature and magic. The plate returns to him, having been breathed on by everyone present. He turns the filled glass upside down onto the plate on the ground, which has new symbols drawn on it. Then, he pours gasoline on the plate and lights it all on fire. We all stare at the fire as if something incredible is about to happen.

The fire burns for a minute or so, then he douses it with water and pulls the glass off and the charcoal ashy substance crumbles into a pile. It appears to be some kind of divination ceremony. Everyone is watching so intensely. My mind wanders.

I think about the lives of the people here and how this Religion, and these kinds of dramatic ceremonies seem to be almost a form of entertainment as much as they are spiritual or religious. I cannot help but wonder how many people here have any idea what's really going on. How much is truly a part of a religious tradition that has been passed down? How much is improvisation? How much is for the impact of suspense and drama, and how much has real significance? When I look around the courtyard, I feel like most of them are more curious than consciously clear about an intention. I think about the roots of this religion, how far back it goes through history and time. I feel the weight of the millions of souls and lives it has touched and moved through. I think about its origins, found deep in the heart and dust of Mother Africa. I contemplate how many thousands of years of evolution it has endured, the oceans it has crossed, the struggles it overcame to find itself alive and embodied now in these particular individuals I am with today.

A wave of profound gratitude washes over me. I feel myself fighting back the tears to stay present. Pure grace pours through me as I recognize how incredibly fortunate I am to be able to witness and participate in this ceremony. The Religion is something truly spectacular, with ancient roots. I am witnessing a form of shamanism and divination that is thousands of years old. I feel beyond blessed.

For several hours the music, dancing, rum drinking and cigar smoking go on, until finally the drummers stop, and cups of hot soup are passed around to nourish and ground everyone. We are all sweating, and exhausted yet happy and fulfilled. Alejandro comes to me and embraces me with a big smile. I asked him what the plate ceremony was all about.

He shrugs his shoulders and laughs. "Nadie sabe, Cheri. Su camino de espíritu es un misterio." (No one really knows. The way of the spirit is a mystery.)

He takes me outside and we sit in the shade with the other drummers and rest. The whole thing is fabulously foreign and fascinating for me. In moments, I wish I was brave enough to film more and document more, but I have such a deep respect for the people and their religion. A ceremony like this is not a public spectacle. This is deep magic and the people here are serious about what is going on, even if they do not fully understand it. They are equally serious about protecting their religion, as they should be. Modern mainstream culture has a way of diluting and polluting everything it touches for commercial reasons, effectively robbing it of its true magic and mystery. I commit to the sanctity of preserving what is sacred as sacred.

New Year's Eve

I am awoken by the heart-stopping sounds of screaming pigs in the yard next to me. It is not yet dawn, and the sound is surreal and disturbing. It goes on for what feels like a long time and forces me out of bed. As I start my day, the sound is echoed from many directions seemingly synchronically, one after the other, the animals calling out in agony, in their last breaths as animal after animal is pierced and bled to death. It is New Year's Eve Day, December 31. I was told that today the streets would run red with the blood of the hundreds of pigs that will be slaughtered for the New Year's feasts. It is not the most humane way to kill an animal by any means. The pigs are bled to death so that the heads are not bruised as the head is one of the delicacies that Cubans enjoy.

In the streets however, I do not actually see blood running, nor do I see any outward signs that today is any different than any other day; yet I know that behind closed doors, the women are working away preparing for the feast. New Year's Eve is a bigger holiday than Christmas for Cubans. It is the night everyone saves for months. The families celebrate at home together with a huge feast which includes roasting a pig, lots of music, dancing and quite often, flowing bottles of rum. It is a full day, and really, a full week of fiesta. Hours at home with the family, neighbors and other family members visiting, and the nights in the discos for the younger ones after full days of drinking and eating.

Yurisney, a close friend of Fernando's, invited me to experience New Year's Eve with his family. Yurisney is small in stature, but with a temper that can explode when agitated or insulted. He is a devoted hard worker. I pass him almost every day in the streets where he works helping tourists to organize their Cuban travel and transit. He has been one of my closest allies when I needed support or friendship in these past few months. I am touched by his invitation knowing that he might just be putting himself in the line of fire with one of his best friends. I also know that there is absolutely nothing but pure friendly sharing in his offer and that he would never disrespect Fernando, nor I, in any way. I appreciate his kind offer, and accept in spite of my nervousness of having more issues with Fernando's insane jealousy.

Yurisney comes for me in the late afternoon and we stroll through the village to his home on the outskirts of the historic district. The barrio is not well maintained, and the clear distinction between the tourist area and the real Trinidad is impossible to miss. The streets are mostly dirt here, the homes are crumbling from the inside out, and yet still the energy is jovial and playful. Yurisney's home is a typical humble Cuban home, but because he works in tourism, things are in a little better condition than many homes here. There is running water in the kitchen and bathroom, and the toilet even has a seat on it and flushes properly. He lives in this two bedroom, one bath home with his mother, his three year old son, his sister, her husband, and his aging grandmother. The concrete floor is adorned with the standard metal and wood furniture that every Cuban lives with, and the two beds are shared amongst them all. Like many Cuban homes in Trinidad, the open-air patio in the back of the house is where much of the cooking and food preparing goes on.

There are huge pots of meats and stews being prepared, a large tray of salad consisting of tomatoes, cucumbers and cabbage, a large pot of congri (black beans and rice) and of course the roasted pork in large trays. We spend the evening dancing, sharing, playing with the kids, and eating for hours. His family is generous and kind, and even with my poor Spanish, and their lack of English, we have a great time conversing, laughing and enjoying the evening together. I feel totally comfortable with them, and like one of the family almost immediately.

New Year's Eve in the states is such a different experience, with so much emphasis on glamor, spending lots of money on a big party, making resolutions and reflecting on the year that has passed. Here, it is such a simple thing, and all about just sharing with family and friends. There is no reflection of past or future whatsoever. It is only enjoying the present moment, and celebrating life in the moment. There is nothing exceptionally special or fancy. There is no need for spending exorbitant amounts of money to show off in fancy clothes with expensive champagnes. It is just a simple sharing of food, time and love to embrace the coming year together.

The hours at Yurisney's house are filled with dancing, and laughter amidst quiet tender moments of conversation and playing with the children. Family members drift in and out with bottles of rum, trays of flan or sweets and lots of smiles, hugs and kisses. His uncle shows up smelling like he's been drenched in gasoline, and insists on dancing with me. I'm repulsed by the smell, but he's such a great dancer, I let myself get past it and the whole family watches and laughs with us as he dips and twirls me around the tiny salon in the front of the house.

The whole barrio is alive with music and laughter.

It's one of the best New Year's Eves I've ever had.

Day of Departure

S*tanding once again* in an airport, a sadness ripples through me. I am returning to a place that I once called home that now feels like a foreign land or some memory of another life far gone. I don't care about shopping and producing. I don't have much interest left for anything of what my culture tries to sell me. I only want to live, share, love, dance, drum, and enjoy the moments passing into more moments.

I feel more like myself, yet suddenly deeply alone for the first time in many months. I know what lies ahead of me is the next phase of letting go of a life that I have lost interest in completely. I know my challenge will be not to fall back into the comfort of the mundane nor the complacency of security and the familiar. I am returning as a different person, a more complete, more raw and real version of myself. I can no longer pretend that living in the way I used to live can ever really be OK for me again.

I do not know what is coming next in my life, but I am holding a vision in my heart. I am living in the possibility that somehow through all of this letting go of my old life, that I will indeed find myself again in Cuba. A dream lives in me and I am not letting it go, not yet. I can't. It's my one little morsel to chew on as I step back into my old life in the USA.

I find my eyes feasting on the darkest-skinned man in the seating area, with his little white cap, and gold jewelry accenting his dark skin so beautifully. I enjoy watching the comfortable way his hand falls between his thighs and cups his crotch. He is regal, and uber sexy. My mind drifts back to Carlos, and for the first time in many months, I wonder how he is doing.

The flight is delayed several hours I know I'm a changed person because it doesn't bother me at all to wait. I've become accustomed to long waits and delays in these three months living in Cuba. The extra hours in the airport are welcomed for me at the moment to give me some time to mentally prepare myself for the culture shock at the end of this flight today. My heart aches. I spend the hours waiting running through memories and moments in my mind. Fernando's face, so perfectly sculpted resting in my arms. The magic of the rhythm and dance and the countless Santería ceremonies, the feel of Oya's breath on my skin and the warmth in my heart can never be taken from me.

I close my eyes and meditate, setting my intention that nothing will stop me from coming back and feeling the Breath of Cuba on my skin again.

Rains of Reality

When I woke up this morning I had no idea where I was. The sound of rain, heavy in my ears greeted me as my eyes slowly peeled open. The room was unfamiliar, sterile and surreal. I stared at the ceiling through a hazy consciousness for some time before closing my eyes again. The beautiful dream I have been living for almost three months is over.

My return to the USA has been a sobering wake up to reality. My return flight was delayed over three hours in Havana making my total wait time at the airport over eight hours. I caught a second round of some kind of flu, and by 8 pm a fever had kicked in. The air conditioner at the airport in Havana was apparently set to "arctic." I had to literally shake myself to stay warm. The Cubans flying back to Miami clearly had plenty of experience with this. They were prepared, and looked quite cozy in their fur collared coats, and bodies draped in fleece blankets.

By the time I arrived in Miami, the rental car company I had reserved with was closed for the night. The options were wait another three hours for the shuttle, then sit and wait for the rental car company to reopen or to pay twice as much for a car from the one company that was still open at 3 am. I chose to pay double and drove myself home at 3 am exhausted and feverish. I put on the Latin music station and made a valiant effort to keep my mind on the music and the driving. I committed to not letting myself feel the emotions that were flooding the edges of my consciousness. At nearly 6 am I arrived at my destination and laid down for a few short hours of sleep. When I awoke, I felt as if I was at the bottom of a deep dark well weeping for my lost world above.

It has been less than twenty-four hours since I left the island. The hole in my heart feels like a valley a million miles wide. Already I am longing for the dances, and the sensual Cuban vibe. Already, I am craving the warm, friendly family feel that is so natural and effortless in Cuba.

Already I am wondering how and when I can get back, and how and when I can finally stay without having to return until I want to. The longing to return is growing like weeds inside of me.

The rain outside echoes the rain in my heart. It comes cascading down in a dramatic downpour of despair. It darkens the night with its dismal duress. My heart is aching. I am lost in culture shock of returning to a life that feels like soggy wet clothes stuck to my body that I cannot peel off no matter how I try.

I do not want to be here. I want to go back to my rock in the Caribbean. I want to return to feel Oya's sweet breath on my skin again. I want to return to that world where it is safe to be seen for who and what I am, where people understand my heart without me having to open my mouth, and where music, friends and dance are reasons enough to live another day.

I do not know how I am going to survive here. I do not want to live here just to *keep on keeping on* in this charade of pretending that living and striving for "The American Dream" is in any way satisfying to my soul or mind.

I feel like a casualty of my culture: a zombie of sorts who has died and come back from the dead as some kind of barely alive skeleton of the *Americana* I never really was. What I really want to do is sell everything I own and run away and never look back. I feel that someday I most certainly will.

I remember my friend Linda who is living full time in Trinidad. I wonder how she finally made the break. I know my story parallels hers in some ways and that she was a reflection for me of a potential future for myself. I wonder what her family thought when she left her homeland for Cuba and gave up all the business of modern life. I wonder if I have the courage to follow suit. I wonder if I really even have a choice. I feel right now like the only choice is find the way to do that, or face a certain death of my soul.

I am more clear than ever before that I do not want to live the rest of my life in the USA. I want to go back to Cuba, and soon. Everything I do now is to find a way to get myself back to the home of my heart. A world where music, dancing and life are one unbroken chain. A place where the heart leads and mind follows. A culture where rhythm, trance and spirit matter. I cannot and will not live the rest of my life here in the USA becoming yet another cog in the wheel of this sickened culture's machine. I just cannot. I will not. It is just not for me.

God, please forgive me for all those I forsake and betray by choosing to live a life that is so purely selfish and soul-filled. Forgive me for leaving my family behind to experience some bliss and joy in this life that none of them have any understanding of whatsoever. Forgive me for pursuing my dreams and for living in alignment with what I truly feel and want.

Forgive me for loving another culture and its ways more than my own. Forgive me for feeling more resonance with people who are not my own, than the blood I was born into. Forgive me for loving the music, the dance, the joy and the passion they infuse my life with, more than money, prestige or fame.

Forgive me that I would choose magic, mystery and the muse over a life of domesticity, children and drudgery.

I want to go home.

Forgive me.

Then please help me find my way home again where The Breath of Cuba can breathe its life through me.

Epilogue

Returning to American culture after my experiences in Cuba was not an easy or graceful transition for me. I slipped in and out of depression. I found myself feeling less and less interested in modern culture and the game of striving for success. My life can never go back to what it was before Cuba, and to be quite honest, I am grateful for it, even as much as it challenges me sometimes.

Everything I learned in Cuba about love and friendship served to make me a more well-rounded and compassionate person. I am eternally grateful for that. The relationships I have had there (and still have) were instrumental in helping me to understand myself, humanity and the Cuban culture in very profound ways. These relationships have also allowed me insight into a kind of love that can withstand drama and return again to acceptance and love in a very familial way. All of the characters in my story are still close friends that I communicate with regularly.

Dancing there has opened me up to new worlds inside of myself and in the community. The gifts of that joyous expression are ever unfolding in my life.

As much as I do not like certain aspects of technology, I am very grateful that I can now communicate more easily and more often with my extended family and friends in Cuba. Most of them now have access to cell phones and data plans. This enables us to stay in touch. The love we have shared is still a part of my daily life today, and I know that all of my Cuban friends will always be a part of my world.

Here is a brief update on their current realities. Remember, Part II was written in 2012, so a lot of time has passed between writing and publication of these memoirs in 2020.

Carlos: From Part I: Havana: My First Cuban Love

Carlos called me within a few hours of my return to the USA in 2012. We met for coffee a few weeks later and laughed about all the craziness that happened in Cuba like old friends. He apologized to me for his bad behavior, and admitted that he was falling in love and it got scary for him. We are still good friends today. More than once we have ended up in Cuba at the same time, and whenever we can, we try to meet up to say hello. I always visit with his family when I am in Havana. Carlos is now married to a lovely woman, and they have two children and live in the midwest of the USA.

Mario: Havana

Mario is still in Havana, and still teaching school for $12 a month. Every time I go to Cuba, I visit with him and his wife. We walk the malecon laughing and reminiscing about the times before cell phones in Cuba. He sometimes assists me with my tours in Cuba and texts me almost every day to check on how I am doing. He is also married to a very intelligent and savvy lawyer in Havana. Together they make less than $50 a month, yet they are happy and grateful for what they have. My clients often bring clothes, and he is one of the people I gift whenever I can.

Ishmael and the Jesus's: Cojimar The Breath of Cuba Part I: My Teachers in Santería

Ishmael has finally entered Facebook, and we are now able to communicate regularly. We chat in text every few days. His health is still good and he is as kind, loving and beautiful as always.

Jesuscito is as skinny as ever but he has finally stopped drinking rum. He tells me when I am there that he does not smoke very much, but he seems to be smoking every time I am there, so I'm not sure how much "not very much" really is. Certainly, his health seems better than it was in 2012. He is still performing and doing ceremonies around the Havana/Alamar region and he sometimes goes to Matanzas for events when called upon.

Jesuscito and Ishmael are always involved in my Signature Tour: The Breath of Cuba Tour. They do small private educational programs to teach my clients about the Religion of Santería in Ishmael's home. The donations my clients bring can sustain them for months at a time. I am so happy to be able to offer some way to give back to them when I can.

Jesus Sr. from Part I, the father of Jesuscito, passed away in 2019 when I was in Cuba. When I went to be with them for the ceremony, everyone talked about how happy he always was and how much love and joy he always shared with everyone who knew him. Jesuscito told me that his father never raised his voice at him, and that he was always cheerful, encouraging and kind to everyone. Read about him in Part I. He was one of the lights of my life in Cojimar, a grandfather figure to me and a truly inspirational composer, percussionist and musician, and he will always live in my heart. In honor of Jesus Limon Morales, they did a very beautiful ceremony and created a lovely altar with photos and keepsakes of his life. (If you visit the archives of my Facebook pages, you can find pictures of the altar. Look in October/November 2019.)

Christina: Trinidad

Christina is now living in Europe with her husband. She misses Cuba a lot. I saw her in 2017, and she had changed considerably. She is already tired and worn down by the modern machine of working too much. She talks often about wanting to return to Cuba. Her mother is doing well and still in Trinidad. We still talk as often as we can, but she does not have a smart phone so it's not as easy to hear her voice as often as I'd like.

Jorge: My Beloved Brother in Music and Dance from Ciego de Ávila

Jorge is now living in Canada, working in construction. He and I text a few times a week. He misses Cuba deeply and returns to Ciego de Ávila every year for a few months to be with his family and work on his home. When he is there, he does not want to return to Canada, but he is the only one in the family earning money to help his mother and family in Cuba.

Fernando: My Love in Trinidad

And last but not least, Fernando, one of the great Cuban dramas of my life. After I left Cuba, we did not talk for some time. I thought about him almost every day, but I didn't really expect anything else to come of it. In the summer of 2012, I went to Europe for a graduate program in Expressive Arts that I was enrolled in. While I was there, he looked me up and begged me to give us another chance. He wanted to meet me in Spain to see how things went outside of Cuba. I loved him, so I went to see him in Spain to test the waters. We had a really beautiful few weeks, but when the same crazy making started again with him, I quickly gathered my things and flew back to the USA. We are still friends and there are no hard feelings between us. I see him almost every time I am in Trinidad as he spends a good bit of time every year in Cuba with his family and daughter. He has gone through multiple relationships, and tells me that European women are "too complicated." That cross-cultural bridge in relationships is clearly not an easy one for him either.

My story is still unfolding and my love affair with Cuba only grows deeper over time. I hope you will keep following the story through my blogs and books as they come out.

Part III of the story will follow this as soon as I can get to it! It will document my experiences post 2015 when I was able to return to the island for my third trip. Post 2015, Cuba is a very different world than when I first went to the island. Cell phones, wifi, data plans, and the influences of these technologies on the minds of Cubans have had dramatic impacts. My trips in 2015 began to open doors for me to begin leading groups and spending more time amongst the Cuban people. In 2017, I sold my belongings and spent the better part of three years in Cuba and what I learned in those years continues to shape who I am becoming as a woman and a human. After I complete the last in this series, I want to publish a fourth book about the nearly three years between 2017-2020 that I spent in Cuba and how my relationship of that time shaped the future of my life.

I'll share an excerpt from Part III here in closing to invite you into the next part of the story.

To book travel to Cuba and support the author:
*go to **www.thebreathofcubatravel.com***

*The author's blog has a rich selection of videos and interviews with Cuban people at **www.thebreathofcuba.com***

Chapter 1 Part 3: The Love Affair Continues

Inevitably, the most challenging departures give way to the 'most beautiful arrivals and openings. Leaving Miami and arriving in Cuba has been one of those inevitabilities. The Cubans in Miami and the Cubans in Cuba are of such a completely different character. One leaves me crying in grief and frustration, the other celebrating spontaneity in the present moment.

The metaphorical reality of letting go of the baggage was so present today. As I walked away from a piece of luggage I delivered from Miami, the magic immediately began unfolding, and now, at 3 am, nearly twelve hours later, I feel worlds away from the place I left behind. The gratitude towards myself for gifting myself this time is rolling through me like a gentle swell far out at sea.

My first few moments alone in the little apartment I rented near Calle Obispo brought me smiling in delight and laughing out loud. A young man in the flat above me was singing at the top of his lungs to Michael Jackson with full enthusiasm. Perhaps I am in the ghetto of Habana, a place some people might turn their noses up at, but here pure joy was erupting above me. I would rather be here than anywhere. Forget the pompous fancy hotels and expensive places. I come to Cuba to be with the people and live amongst them. I come here to feel the pure innocence of having nothing and celebrating everything.

My night was led by the gods it seems. The moment I stepped foot on the streets, the magic started. The energy here is just indescribably effortless for me to sink into. It's tender, pure, innocent and powerfully passionate. It's home like no other place on earth has been to me somehow.

When I strolled onto Calle Obispo, the first thing I noticed was the difference in the last time I was here in 2012. A long row of people were leaning against a storefront staring intently at their cell phones and tablets. Clearly this was a wifi spot. "Wifi tarjeta senorita" a man called out to me, and I just smiled and kept walking. Next to him, another young man who had scars on his face and interesting eyes, caught my attention. My first feeling was apprehension, but something in me told me to stop and inquire about the cards, and there the magic started.

As Cubans often are, he was very open and talkative. His name is Angel. We quickly entered into a discussion that went from the wifi cards, to my travels in Cuba before. That led to a whole evening of sharing. I have now met four of his six brothers, and his mother, and spent hours walking the streets with him just talking and connecting, as well as an hour chilling at his place with the family, watching TV. His mother is close to my age, and at fifty looks amazing. He must be in his late twenties, but to be honest, he looks older than she does. Life for him, I can see, has not been easy. The scars on his face and the shape of his eyes, likely from a beating of some kind, don't hide his past well.

More interesting and magical is the depth to which the connection goes. His mother, Nurika, just happens to be friends with Ishmael, my padrino and friend from my first trip in 2010, as well as my music teacher Jesus Morales. What are the chances that my first night back on the island in three years would bring me to a scar-faced kid whose mother is good friends with the first friends I made in Cuba over five years ago? Of all the millions of people in Havana, I was led directly to people who are of the same family of heart. I was sharing with them some videos of my drumming and when I showed her, she immediately suggested we go together to a ceremony and dance.

At 11 pm I came back to my place to change, and at 11:30 I found myself sitting quietly alone on the step by the street, just watching the world go by the way Cubans do for hours a day. It felt good to just sit on the stoop and watch people walk by. A woman walking alone saw me, and came to talk to me. She was intrigued that I was just sitting there, and wanted to know why I was there alone. She was a lovely woman, very interesting and someone I hope I see again to spend more time with.

Now I am exhausted, my first night back in Cuba for over three years, and I am already filled with so much love and sweetness. I feel the weight of the world dropping from my shoulders, and I think perhaps it is truly time to simplify my life and get back to what matters. For the next month, at least, that's all I'm here to do. Live, love, laugh, enjoy, dance, walk, chat, practice my Spanish, catch up on some writing and enjoy beautiful Cuba for all it has to offer before it is ruined and changed forever.